JOHN THE BAPTIST

A Lenten Pilgrimage Through Art

JERRY CAMERY-HOGGATT

AMESTOY HILL PUBLISHERS
Granada Hills, CA

Scripture quotations are from the Revised Standard Version of the Bible,
copyright © 1971 or from the New Revised Standard Version Bible,
copyright © 1989, by the Division of Christian Education of the National
Council of Churches of Christ in the USA.
Used by permission. All rights reserved.

Cover art by
John Nava
Baptism of the Lord
Used with Permission, Copyright 2003
John Nava/The Cathedral of Our Lady of the Angels

Dedication

For
RUTH AND MICHAEL GODDERZ
Who taught me the meaning of grace

And for
H. KEITH EWING
Who taught me to love both art and poetry

ᚼ

Contents

Introduction

The season of Lent has always been a time for reflection on the meaning of Christian faith, and for shedding all that is incompatible or distracting from the practice of that faith. For over fifteen hundred years Christians have observed Lent by taking pilgrimage; those who were able would travel to Jerusalem or to other sites in the Holy Land.

In the Middle Ages, when Crusaders returned with mementos of their journeys or with relics of the saints, they began to set up shrines for the faithful who had been unable to travel. These eventually developed into the well-known Stations of the Cross, commonly represented in paintings or sculptures upon which the faithful could meditate as they made their own local pilgrimages in quest of deeper spirituality. A stationary pilgrimage is a fundamental shift. Or is it? Rather, it points up the reality that the Lenten pilgrimage is an interior journey rather than a merely physical one, and that the physical places to which one might travel may be less important than the spiritual landscape within.

The point of a pilgrimage is prayer and piety.

Still, there's a fundamental difference between visiting an actual holy place, as it was in history perhaps, and visiting the "same" place represented in the various media of art: the artists add an additional something to the images; within the images they layer in their own quest for holiness, or relevance, or fame even. The "places" they represent are set within the byways and stopping places of their own internal and spiritual landscapes.

This essay on John the Baptist takes its inspiration from this same practice. I offer pausing places along the route of John's life upon which we might ponder together the nature of the holiness he demanded and expected, and the holiness of the One whose way John had come to prepare.

His very life expresses what he once answered in response to a question from a disciple: "He must increase, but I must decrease." As difficult as it was, the life of the Baptist has very much to say to us during the holy season of Lent. Perhaps more than anyone else, in his message and ministry he reminds us that all things are subordinate to the Messiah whom he serves.

John's life also speaks to us of the importance of complete, unflinching renunciation, of declaring for God, of taking God seriously — at all times, in all places. His was a life in the wilderness, an uncomfortable life, doing the work of God at enormous personal cost.

So John's story is an Example Story, meant to tell us in graphic form that the life of the Kingdom is a life of sacrifice. As we will see in the images that follow, John too must have had his Temptation in the Wilderness, his moment of crisis and decision. As do we. There are many kinds of deserts, many places where we may feel abandoned or bereft, and the psychological or spiritual wildernesses may confront us with our own need to decide, once and for all, whom we will serve.

Considering such questions is at the heart of the Lenten pilgrimage, and as we ponder them, we may take both clarity and courage from the example of John who preceded us. If we listen carefully, we too may hear John's thundering "Prepare ye the way of the Lord" as an invitation to Lenten contemplation, to studied seriousness about the practice of our faith, and — perhaps now more than ever — to respond to John's perennial call to repent, "for the Kingdom of God is at hand."

JERRY CAMERY-HOGGATT

John
the Baptist
A Lenten pilgrimage through art

Do not be afraid Zechariah, for your prayer has been heard. Your wife Elizabeth will bear you a son, and you will name him John.

James Tissot
Jerusalem
1886-1894 | opaque watercolor on graphite over gray woven paper
8 1/4 x 17 1/16 inches | Brooklyn Museum

The Angel Appears
to Zechariah

Most of our pilgrimage will take us to villages and desert haunts, but the story itself opens in Jerusalem, within the massive temple complex, within the temple, within the sacred enclosure of the temple. French Bible illustrator James Tissot (1836-1902) has recreated the wider context for us in this gouache watercolor, painted as part of a series of three hundred, fifty pieces reconstructing the life of Jesus. Tissot is credited with being the first artist whose work paid painstaking attention to the archeological evidence that was available at the time.

Andrea Pisano
The Angel Appears to Zechariah
1330-1336 | bronze bas relief | 49.7 x 43.2 cm
The Baptistery of the Cathedral | Florence

It is what is happening inside the temple that captures our attention. For that, we turn to one of the panels that grace the doors of the baptistery of the Florence Cathedral. The panel is by Andrea Pisano (1295-1348), and it, too is part of a series, this one containing twenty gilded bronze *bas relief* panels depicting the life of John. The old man Zechariah is serving as priest before the altar when his work is interrupted by a visitation from the angel Gabriel, who appears beside the altar, his right hand raised in greeting. Zechariah blanches at the sight, but is reassured: "Do not be afraid, Zechariah, for your prayer has been heard. Your wife Elizabeth will bear you a son, and you will name him John."

Domenico Ghirlandaio
The Angel appears to Zechariah
1486-1490 | fresco | Santa Maria Novella | Florence

I talian artist Domenico Ghirlandaio (1449–1494) sets the scene within the chancel of a Christian cathedral; Zechariah is celebrating mass when the angel appears, this time resplendent in his rainbow colored wings.

Art critics have often remarked on the lines of dignitaries who have assembled here, no doubt at the insistence of the patron who funded the work. Historically such a grouping is probably impossible; while offering sacrifice within the sacred precinct of the temple, Zechariah would have been alone, and there would have been no one to observe the exchange with the angel. Yet in a sense we are there, too, vicarious participants in a profoundly holy and significant moment. Through the medium of the biblical narrative, we are allowed to overhear the angel, and to share Zechariah's consternation.

The angel has made his appearance. Zechariah, startled, looks up from his ministrations. For a moment he is on hallowed ground, represented not only by the altar, but also by his bare feet. One is reminded of the voice Moses once heard from the burning bush in the book of Exodus:

> "Put off your shoes from your feet, for the place on which you are standing is holy ground."

The angel speaks only to him:

> "Do not be afraid, Zechariah, for your prayer has been heard. Your wife Elizabeth will bear you a son, and you will name him John. You will have joy and gladness, and many will rejoice at his birth, for he will be great in the sight of the Lord. He must never drink wine or strong drink; even before his birth he will be filled with the Holy Spirit. He will turn many of the people of Israel to the Lord their God. With the spirit and power of Elijah he will go before him, to turn the hearts of parents to their children, and the disobedient to the wisdom of the righteous, to make ready a people prepared for the Lord."

The anguish in Zechariah's voice is palpable: "How will I know that this is so? For I am an old man, and my wife is getting on in years." It is an understandable hesitation; he and Elizabeth have tried for children for decades. They are righteous, God-fearing people, and yet this blessing has eluded them.

6

The observers in the nave seem unaware. Several are engaged in conversation, and none of the eyes are trained on the angel. They are there but they are not there. So Zechariah and the angel are alone after all. Ghirlandaio is signaling us from the 15th Century that one may well be influential enough to insist on being painted into a holy scene, but that does not make one holy. Elizabeth Barrett Browning was right: Earth may indeed be crammed with heaven, and yet only those who see take off their shoes.

Do not be afraid
Zechariah,
for your prayer
has been heard.
Your wife Elizabeth
will bear you a son,
and you will name him
John.

On the surface of it, the angel's response to Zechariah seems less than kind. For this we return to the work of the Nineteenth Century French watercolorist James Tissot. The angel rises slowly, hovering, preparing for his departure:

"I am Gabriel," he says. "I stand in the presence of God, and I have been sent to speak to you and to bring you this good news. But now, because you did not believe my words, which will be fulfilled in their time, you will become mute, unable to speak, until the day these things occur."

James Tissot
The Angelic visit to Zechariah
1886-1894 | opaque watercolor over graphite on
gray woven paper
Museum of Art | Brooklyn

8

He reaches out with his left hand and touches Zechariah on the lips, sealing the deal.

It is an odd way to depart. Good news, a failed test, a fresh trial. What does this tell us of the Gospel? Perhaps that we, like Zechariah, are asked to trust, to hold fast to the promises of God even when we do not understand how they might come to pass, and that in the absence of trust we may find ourselves tongue-tied, disabled participants in the work that God is doing to redeem the world.

Do not be afraid
Zechariah,
for your prayer
has been heard.
Your wife **Elizabeth**
will bear you a son,
and you will name him
John.

In the sixth month,
The angel **Gabriel**
was sent
                    by
       God
to a virgin.
The virgin's name was
                Mary.

In the sixth month,
The angel **Gabriel**
was sent *by*
God
to a virgin.
The virgin's name was
Mary.

The Annunciation to Mary

One can hardly tell the story of John in the absence of the story of Jesus, and so we turn aside briefly and report an important moment in the major plot that gives John's sub-plot its meaning: the visit of the angel Gabriel to Jesus' mother Mary. It may seem strange to consider the Annunciation in relation to Lent — the Annunciation is commonly connected with Advent. There are good reasons nonetheless. Not least of these is the fact that the Feast of the Annunciation falls on March 25th, nine months before Christmas, and thus during Lent. And at least in the Gospel of St Luke, this moment forms a foundation for much of the gospel narrative that follows. It foregrounds the rest of the narrative by establishing the theological framework in which the lives of both Jesus and John are to be understood.

When actor Mel Gibson was interviewed about his film, *The Passion of the Christ*, one of the interviewers asked him who was responsible for the death of Jesus. "I am," he said. "We all are." It was a specific kind of truth-claim, one that cannot be validated by any empirical evidence, but only by a movement of faith. The questioner was asking an *historical* question; Gibson answered with a theological response. In this we find two differing planes of experience, one earthbound and physical, the other transcendent and spiritual.

Matter and Spirit. One is visible to the naked eye, the other visible only to the eye of faith.

The challenge of the Christian artist is to represent the intersection of these two planes. This is no easy task, as art historian Neil MacGregor reminds us:

> Making an image of God who has become man is . . . a tricky

13

business. Artists attempting it have to negotiate a series of specifically visual problems, unknown to authors. Paradox is easy to write, but hard to paint. The Gospel tells us quite straightforwardly that the helpless, swaddled infant is in reality God incarnate, but how do you *show* that it is God in nappies, that the purpose of this child is to redeem the world by his death?

In the sixth month
The angel Gabriel
was sent by
God
to a virgin.
The virgin's name was
Mary.

S ometimes a single detail is enough to do the trick. In 1838, the Austrian painter Joseph von Fuhrich (1800-1876) gave us a painting entitled *The Arrival of the Holy Family in Front of the Inn at Bethlehem*. It is a typical rejection scene, not unlike what one sees on display each year in the stationery stores. Mary sits sidesaddle on her donkey; Joseph approaches the door. The inn-keeper appears in the window with a dismissive gesture: "Go away, the inn is full."

Joseph von Fuhrich
The Arrival of the Holy Family in front of the Inn at Bethlehem
1838 | Staatliche Museen | Berlin

Behind and above the Holy Couple a band of revelers sits on a terrace, pouring libations and singing to the accompaniment of a man with a lute. What distinguishes this picture  is the sign above the door giving the name of the inn: MUNDUS — *world*. With this single detail, von Fuhrich has turned the entire scene into a theological commentary, a visual echo of St John's famous prologue:

> He was in the world, and the world was made through him, yet the world knew him not. He came to his own home, and his own people received him not.

The indifference of the revelers above suddenly takes on another meaning, and we find ourselves scrutinizing their behavior: In their frivolities they are living wholly on the physical plane, and so missing completely the holy, redemptive story that is playing out in the courtyard beneath them.

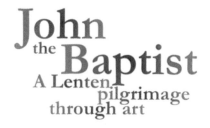

John the Baptist
A Lenten pilgrimage through art

Philippe de Champaigne
The Annunciation
c.1644 | oil on panel | 28 x 28.75 inches
Metropolitan Museum of Art | New York City

A different artistic strategy is to pack the pictures with symbols, called *emblems* in the artistic tradition. Over time, the emblems acquired a kind of fixedness, and so became a language. Martyrs and others who suffered great loss are depicted in red; saints wear haloes; white indicates purity or holiness. Mary Magdalene carries an ointment jar; St Paul carries a walking staff.

A good example is *The Annunciation*, by the French artist Philippe de Champaigne (1602-1674). To modern eyes the scene appears overly sentimental. An idealized Mary is approached by an idealized angel; a playful covey of cherubs looks on from above. The dove of the Holy Spirit descends upon her, riding a beam of light. Everything is safe, painted in pastels.

We are helped to see this scene the way the artist intended if we think of this as a kind discourse, but delivered in the vocabulary of religious symbolism. Mary wears both blue and red--the red tunic signifying suffering, the blue signaling royalty, a fitting color for the Queen of Heaven. She is Queen, not by virtue of birth or marriage, but because she is the mother of the King. As is common in portrayals of this scene, Mary is shown kneeling in prayer. Thus the viewer knows that the book she is reading is a prayer book. The open cabinet reveals two other books, one large and trimmed in gold, latched by two golden clasps. It is no doubt the Holy Scriptures. The books indicate that she is a woman of piety and learning. The angel bears a lily, the symbol of peace, indicating visually that he intends her no harm.

But there is a chance that this scene may be misread. Pastel angels with lilies in their hands may be overly comfortable — charming messengers with sweet messages. The news Gabriel brings for Mary is something other, an earth-shattering promise that will bring her world crashing down around her. It comes from a fiercely holy God intent on bringing reconciliation with fallen humanity at all costs; what the angel does not tell her is that the costs will be exorbitant.

Ecce ancilla Domini.
Behold the handmaid of the Lord.

Henry Ossawa Tanner
The Annunciation
1898 | oil on canvas | 57 x 71 ½ in.
Museum of Art | Philadelphia

American artist Henry Ossawa Tanner (1859-1937), moves us almost to the opposite extreme, depicting everything just as it might have appeared. Tanner is often considered a master of the Realist school of art, focusing on the homely details of actual scenes. Mary is dressed simply, and the scene is devoid of emblems. The hint of an arch above her suggests the contours of an ordinary room.

The exception here is in the depiction of the angel. What sort of Realist paints angels? (Gustave Coubert, one of the earliest and most influential exponents of the Realist school, is reported to have said, in effect, "Show me an angel, and I will paint an angel.") But Tanner has tried, and there are some who might claim that he has failed. Let us consider this. By definition, angels are emissaries, deliverers of divine messages. This angel will open his monologue with an affirmation:

"Hail, Mary, full of grace, the Lord is with thee."

But still Mary is frightened, opening reassurances notwithstanding. We tend to suppose that she is frightened by the implications of the message, but those are not yet spelled out. Tanner supplies us with another perspective: she is overwhelmed by the holiness, which appears as an intense flame. Is not holiness like that? A consuming fire?

Tanner has captured the moment a short time after Mary has awakened. She does not yet know what has disturbed her sleep; perhaps she is still dreaming. She swings her legs free of the bedclothes and sits up. It dawns on her that something is in the room. She gazes at the light, her expression perplexed but patient. Her hands rest easily on her lap. She does not yet know that she is in the presence of an angel. How could she? It will take a moment for the flame to cool and the angel's features to appear.

She is entirely present.

Behold the handmaid of the Lord.

20

James Tissot
The Annunciation
1886-1894 | gouache | 17 x 21.7 cm
Museum of Art | Brooklyn

James Tissot provides a strikingly different take on the Annunciation, to a strikingly different effect. While Tanner's angel is flaming yellow, fiery and intense, Tissot's is a cool cobalt blue; while Tanner's is all flame, Tissot's is all feathers. Tanner has  dressed his Mary in ordinary clothes — he was a realist, after all — but Tissot has followed custom and smothered her in bolts and bolts of white cloth, emblematic of purity. Mary reacts differently as well. We have caught them at different moments in the dialogue.

The giveaway in Tissot's piece is the odd, nearly impossible lay of the cloth. At first glance it appears that Mary has backed against the wall and fallen to her knees, but if that were so how would the cloth come to be arranged in that way, drawn out in front of her rather than crumpled beneath? So closer observation suggests that she has only just now risen from a prostrate position, face-down on the mat, drawing the cloth back as she rises. She has been on her face in the presence of the holy. The vision in the room is terrifying, no less so than the flame in Tanner's portrayal, but the intense heat has cooled, and the angel has reassured her:

"Do not be afraid, Mary, for you have found favor with God."

She draws herself up, settles on her knees, but continues to avert her eyes. What the angel says next is impossible: "And now, you will conceive in your womb and bear a son, and you will name him Jesus." Tissot asks us to imagine Mary answering with her head low and her eyes still averted, a posture that makes it difficult to imagine her voice as anything larger than a whisper:

"How can this be, since I am a virgin?"

Gabriel clarifies. Mary listens with her head bowed, her eyes still averted. She can barely speak, and her hands are open before her in a mute but eloquent gesture of receptivity. In the silent medium of his paints, Tissot has signaled her final response — spoken so low we can barely hear it:

"Behold the handmaid of the Lord. Be it unto me according to thy word."

There is a subtlety here that we must not miss: when Zechariah questioned the angel, he was struck mute, a kind of angelic lesson not to repeat the same error twice. When Mary questions, she is offered reassurance and the confirming evidence of family:

> "The Holy Spirit will come upon you, and the power of the Most High will overshadow you; therefore the child to be born will be holy; he will be called Son of God. And now, your relative Elizabeth in her old age has also conceived a son; and this is the sixth month for her who was said to be barren."

So Gabriel has grown more compassionate.

Mary will need this added tenderness. The angel has asked very much of her, and there is ample evidence in the gospels that what he promises in return will elude her for most of her life. Her reputation will be ruined; indeed, rumors of infidelity will still infest the neighborhood thirty years later when the authorities in Jerusalem send people to investigate Jesus. The Gospel of John reports the authorities taunting him: "We're not the ones who were born of fornication," implying in their diction that he was. The taunt disparages him, but it also disparages his mother. Once he starts stirring the religious and political pot, her family will fragment over what to do about him; the neighbors, or perhaps his siblings, will say that he has lost his mind. And in the end, she will live to see him strung up like a common criminal and left to die.

Ecce ancilla Domini.

Behold the handmaid of the Lord.

But visitations from angels are notoriously hard to forget, and as she watches the realities of Jesus' life, they will clash with the promises the angel has made.

The angel had promised: "He will be called the Son of God." But before this story is concluded, she will hear the taunts of the authorities:

"*We're* not the ones born of fornication here . . . ."

The angel had promised: "He will establish the Kingdom of his father David." But before the story is concluded she will see him crowned with thorns and strung up on a cross to die, with a placard above his head that reads,

"THE KING OF THE JEWS."

The angel had promised: "Of his kingdom there shall be no end." But before the story is concluded she will watch his life ebb from him, his labored breathing at the end of his life echoing hers at the beginning of it.

The angel had promised: "The Lord God will give to him the throne of his ancestor David." But in the moments just before his passing she will hear his cry of dereliction from the cross:

"*Eloi, Eloi, lama sabachthani?*"

"My God, my God, why hast thou forsaken me?"

Is it not likely that Mary would echo this same cry from the depths of her own broken heart?

The promise and the reality read like a horrible, ironic litany; the incarnation that began with an unexpected, blessed birth is carried to its inevitable, heartrending conclusion. It is difficult not to imagine Mary seeing all of this and hearing all of this, and wondering how the promises of the angel could come to such a horrific end. It seems savage enough to tear a sensitive soul apart.

This is the mystery Mary must manage to resolve: in the end, how does she reconcile the promises of a trustworthy God with the unspeakable horror of the crucifixion of her son? But like the promise, the mystery Mary will struggle to understand and accept is a mystery that puzzles us all. On a smaller scale, this is our mystery, too; she puzzles on our behalf. How do we reconcile the inevitable losses of life with the life-giving promises of a redemptive God?

In this way the images bring us back to the two planes of existence, one earthly and human, the other transcendent and spiritual, and they ask us to believe that the transcendent reality is the encompassing context in which the earthly reality should be understood. In one of his epistles to the Corinthians St Paul provides a clue: In the absence of faith, the workings of the cross are sheer lunacy; in the presence of faith, they are the redemptive power of a loving God. In the absence of faith, the promises the angel made to Mary are worse than mistaken; they are cruel lies told to a woman of depth and piety. What kind of God plays such jokes on the people that he loves?

But perhaps we should read this in another way. Suppose Mary had never had the visitation of an angel, and thus had no transcendent framework in which to view the tragic events of the passion? Would that not lead to despair? Could it be that the visit from the angel at the beginning of the journey was a preparation for the difficulties and tragedies she would face at the end?

He has offered her the gift of a transcending vision, and thus a source of serenity in the coming season of sacrifice.

John
the
Baptist
A Lenten pilgrimage
through art

A nd did she find that serenity? Perhaps we can find the answer by fast-forwarding to the end, picking up Mary's story with Michelangelo's (1475-1564, Italy) *Pietà*.

Michelangelo
Pietà
1499 | marble | 68.5 in x 76.8 in
St Peter's Basilica | Vatican City

Ecce ancilla Domini.
Behold the handmaid of the Lord.

What is most striking about this image is the Madonna's youthfulness; she is barely a teenager here, holding her dead son. Though her face is filled with sorrow, it remains completely unmarred by even this great tragedy. How do we explain that? Michelangelo's own reported answer: "She has stayed young because she has stayed pure."

It is traditional to think of Mary's purity as perfect sexual purity, but an argument could be made that the term has a wider range of meanings. Mary is pure of heart, a purity rooted in her unadulterated trust in the faithfulness of God.

C. S. Lewis once remarked that he believed in God the way he believed in the sun, not because he had seen the sun but because in the sun's light all other things could be seen aright. That, of course, is the way Mary managed to survive the catastrophes of her life, including the death of her beloved son. She reverses the order of things, reads the tragedy in the light of the promise rather than the other way around.

So perhaps these images ask us to reverse the order of our expectations. Instead of the reality giving the lie to the promises of God, the promises of God somehow give the lie to the finality of the trouble. It is the promises of God, pure and simple, that sustain her even when all of the visible evidence seems to run in the opposite direction.

In the reality of the promises of God, Mary has been blessed with a transcending grace.

In those days
Mary set out
and went with haste
to a Judaean town in the hill country,
where she entered the house
of Zechariah
&
Elizabeth

John
the
Baptist
A Lenten
pilgrimage
through art

The Visitation of Mary to Elizabeth

The angel has told Mary that her relative Elizabeth is also with child — an astonishing claim since Mary would know of Elizabeth's barrenness and her advanced age. She will follow the cue and make the trip to Judea. No doubt she had other reasons for such a trip. Perhaps Elizabeth will need her help. Perhaps with so much at stake, she herself needs reassurance.

The Visitation of Mary to Elizabeth is one of the most celebrated encounters in the history of art — as it should be. It is a moment of great importance in the biblical story, a symbolic meeting of two worlds. Jesus will later tell us that John was the greatest of the old world, the greatest of those born of women, and yet — Jesus will also say — even the least in the kingdom is greater than he. The saying is not meant to minimize John, but rather to emphasize the wholly new thing that God is doing in the Kingdom of Heaven. John is greater than the prophets. Greater than Moses, even. But what is happening with the advent of the new "Kingdom that is Coming" is greater still, greater even than all of that.

The book of Hebrews casts this shift in dramatic terms:

> In many and various ways God spoke of old to our fathers by the prophets; but in these last days he has spoken to us by a Son, whom he appointed the heir of all things, through whom also he created the world.

The time will come when John will take his place among the prophets.

Like him, they foregrounded and prepared the way for the Christ. Like him, in their own ways they announced the Kingdom of Heaven, demanded justice, spoke truth to power, and yet he surpassed them all in this: He embodied the prophetic tradition that looked forward to the day of redemption.

When the angel appeared to Zechariah in the temple, his message included a promise that John would come "in the spirit and power of Elijah, to turn the hearts of parents to their children, and the disobedient to the wisdom of the righteous, to make ready a people prepared for the Lord." The birth of John fulfills not only that promise, but the promise that had come from the pen of Malachi:

> "Behold, I will send you Elijah the prophet before the great and terrible day of the LORD comes. And he will turn the hearts of fathers to their children and the hearts of children to their fathers. . . ."

John is, in his own flesh, the very announcement he has come to make; it is literally built into his DNA. And so his very birth "prepares the way of the Lord." He is at once the closing crescendo of the old song and the opening prelude of the new.

In their efforts to grasp that importance, the artists have layered in overlapping and complementary themes in their portrayals of this scene — the old and the new, the old covenant and the new covenant, the old woman and the young woman, disgrace reclaimed, and blessing announced.

The viewer knows that grace will triumph, and that the purposes of God will outrun the capriciousness of conventional wisdom. Both births will be miraculous, and both children will be set apart for some divine purpose, agents of judgment and grace.

This is what Mary has come to confirm — a promise made specifically to her, but which has ramifications for the world. If Elizabeth is pregnant, the angel's promise is good. We hold our breath as she undertakes this difficult embassage.

In those days
Mary set out
and went with haste
to a Judaean town in the hill country,
where she entered the house
of Zechariah
&
Elizabeth

John the Baptist

A Lenten pilgrimage through art

In this watercolor by James Tissot, Mary has just arrived. The angel has not told her about the angelic visit to Zechariah, and so she has no way to know how they will understand this apparently illicit pregnancy. Will they believe her story about the angel and the virginal conception? It is a moment of deep hesitation, freighted with dangers. In this painting she is smaller, more diminutive, more in need of the sheltering protection of her older cousin. What if she is

rejected here? Where will she turn? Will Elizabeth even understand the import of her own pregnancy? Mary's face reflects the gravity of the situation.

Elizabeth shows herself not unaware of the possibility of prying eyes and raised eyebrows among the neighbors. She whisks the girl into the protective enclave of the courtyard. Tongues will wag; the village gossips will have their field day. In the villages of Judea, as in villages everywhere, everybody knows everybody's business, including — especially — the moral missteps.

James Tissot
The Visitation
1886-1894 | opaque watercolor on woven paper
6 7/8 x 4 5/8 in.
Museum of Fine Arts | Brooklyn

Someone with a donkey follows behind. Could it be that Joseph has taken time to see her safely to family? He is an old man here — a traditional conclusion drawn from his disappearance from the biblical narrative. It is little wonder that he lags behind. Who knows what the girl's family will think when they arrive unannounced, with Mary pregnant and showing?

Whatever her first impressions, Elizabeth draws the girl inside, while Zechariah hangs back to close the gate after the entourage is safe within.

John the Baptist
A Lenten pilgrimage through art

In this portrayal by William-Adolphe Bouguereau (1825-1905, France) the two women pause to take stock. Perhaps because of Mary's halo, Elizabeth recognizes that she is in the presence of holiness.

To everyone's surprise, it is Elizabeth who needs reassurance from Mary. Her age shows in this image. She is frail, gaunt even. Her back is not straight, but bowed by the weight of a long life without children, and thus without standing in the community. Mary's tender gesture is reassuring. There is very much happening, all of it beyond understanding, but all of it from God nonetheless.

If Joseph holds back here too, we can understand why: He is no doubt wondering what Elizabeth must be thinking. Introductions will come in a moment, but he knows that on the surface of it, things look bad. He is old

William-Adolphe Bouguereau
La Visitation
1876
La chapelle de la Vierge
Cathédrale de Saint-Louis,
Poitou-Charentes
La Rochelle | France

37

enough to be the girl's father. Elizabeth will surely know that they are not yet married, and it would be reprehensible for a man of his age to take advantage of an impressionable teenage girl, in another day a capital offense.

He waits, allowing the women whatever time they need, yet remains close enough to come to Mary's assistance should she be rejected here, too, as — perhaps — she has been rejected already in Nazareth. Who knows what Mary's family will think of this apparently illicit pregnancy? Her cousin is married to a priest who serves in the temple, and among such people moral convictions run both cold and deep.

In those days
Mary set out
and went with haste
to a Judaean town in the hill country,
where she entered the house
of Zechariah
&
Elizabeth

Domenico Ghirlandaio
The Visitation
c. 1491 | tempera on wood
172 x 165 cm
The Louvre | Paris

In the end, like Mary, Elizabeth is also blessed with transcending grace. In this piece, by the Florentine artist Domenico Ghirlandaio (1449-1494), she is overcome by the holiness of the moment, and she literally kneels before her younger relative. It is a family affair, but Joseph and Zechariah have left the women so they can talk alone; perhaps they are seeing to the donkey; perhaps they are making their own peace. The two cousins are attended by other women, friends perhaps, or servants. Mary's attendant appears also to be sympathetically pregnant. Elizabeth's has her hands folded as if in prayer, though the gesture may be more natural — an expression of concern for the Mistress' well-being.

It is a time of deep uncertainty for Mary, though her face appears serene in this picture. Elizabeth is alert to that dimension of the moment and offers what are surely the most reassuring words Mary can hear: ""Blessed are you among women, and blessed is the fruit of your womb."

For Mary it is a moment of great relief. She is safe.

In those days
Mary set out
and went with haste
to a Judaean town in the hill country,
where she entered the house
of Zechariah
&
Elizabeth

She need not have worried. Elizabeth's concern is all for her, as we discover in this piece by the consummate Mannerist, Jacopo Pontormo (1494-1557). Whatever the neighbors might think, Elizabeth herself has no doubts. Mary is blessed, Elizabeth says, "for as soon as I heard the sound of your greeting, the child in my womb leaped for joy." Even before his birth, John has begun his ministry.

Jacopo Pontormo
The Visitation
1528-29 | oil on wood
202 x 156 cm
San Michele Carmignano
Florence

Elizabeth is stronger here, her spirits buoyed by the confirmation she has felt inside herself. The two attendants stand at attention, faces grave, ready to respond if they are needed. Pontormo has countered the solemnity of the occasion by painting the scene in the monumental figures and exuberant colors of the Mannerist style that followed the Renaissance in Italy. While the colors are exuberant, the faces of the women are solemn: "Here, let me look at you."

There is an urgent exchange of news. Elizabeth is also pregnant, already showing, which adds physical confirmation to the blessing and the promise Mary had heard from the visiting angel Gabriel:

> "The Holy Spirit will come upon you, and the power of the Most High will overshadow you; therefore the child to be born will be holy; he will be called Son of God. And now, your relative Elizabeth in her old age has also conceived a son; and this is the sixth month for her who was said to be barren."

But the promise that all will be well is not without pains of its own. Though Elizabeth's disgrace has been taken from her, Mary surely realizes that hers has only just begun. The village wags in Nazareth will have their say, and there will be no protective covering of family where she will be free of prying eyes and clucking tongues. In the painful years ahead, when the gossips in Nazareth will question Mary's purity and fidelity to her husband, she will remember these words of reassurance — terms of endearment — from an elder in the clan, and find some comfort there. So this is a moment of both solemnity and great joy. The two women reach for each other reflexively, their touches both tender and tentative. Grace and disgrace mingle together, trading places.

In those days
Mary set out
and went with haste
to a Judaean town in the hill country,
where she entered the house
of Zechariah
&
Elizabeth

42

Mariotto Albertinelli (1474-1515, Italy), catches the two women in another embrace.

Mariotto Albertinelli
The Visitation
1503 | oil on wood | 91 x 57 ½ in
Galleria Uffizi | Florence

It is difficult to date this image. Has Mary just arrived? Or is this the final farewell before they part company, perhaps for the last time? St Luke tells us that Mary stayed with Elizabeth for three months before she returned home. Why leave then? Perhaps it is because travel was dangerous for a pregnant woman, even with an attendant, or perhaps the weather was about to turn, and the roads would become impassable. Joseph is nowhere to be found; has he returned already to Nazareth to see to the family's business? Luke does not say.

The two attendants have thoughtfully left the scene; perhaps the one is cleaning up and the other packing for the journey home. For Mary, now visibly pregnant, the return journey will be more arduous than the one that brought her here, and the circumstances in Nazareth promise to be less safe and reassuring than what she has found in Elizabeth's tender embrace and the murmured words of affirmation. She knows that in her wedding to Joseph the pregnancy will be visible beneath her gown, and that there will be very few in Nazareth — perhaps no one — who would believe her story about the angel. Even so, she wears now the blue of royalty. The red dress showing beneath the mantel is Albertinelli's nod to the tragic loss she will experience in the death of her child.

He has set the scene before a monumental arch, a passageway to the next phases of the story. Mary will leave us shortly because the story we are following belongs to Elizabeth. And yet her presence will linger behind in the viewer's eye, a fitting symbolic backdrop to the birth of John. It is Mary's son who gives Elizabeth's son the meaning of his life.

Now the time came for Elizabeth to give birth.

John the Baptist

A Lenten pilgrimage through art

The Birth of John

Andrea Pisano
The Birth of the Baptist
1330-1336 | bronze bas relief | 49.7 x 43.2 cm
The Baptistery of the Cathedral, Florence, Italy

In this scene we return to Pisano's *bas reliefs* on the south facing doors of the Baptistery of the Florence cathedral. Here, as with the other images on the doors, everything is solid, immortalized in a series of snap-shot moments, hardly changed after nearly eight

47

hundred years. Such is the enduring power of Pisano's bronze medium. Pisano's work is noted for its restraint, the careful placement of the figures within controlled compositions, the finely honed attention to detail. It is such qualities that make a work of art immortal, and so ironically they point beyond the solidity of the medium to a more spiritual reality that cannot be captured in bronze, or marble, or oil, but can only be evoked in the heart of the viewer.

It is these tiny movements of empathy within the heart of the viewer that remind us that the real moment of Elizabeth's triumph was chancier, more dangerous. The way St Luke tells the story, Elizabeth is an old woman, and though the pregnancy had its origins in divine Providence, still she must have experienced the pregnancy and delivery as freighted with dangers; could it be that the infant will survive the birth, but that she will not? Such things are known to happen even to younger women. But she is righteous, a woman of prayer, and there has been a prophecy. What the angel is telling her is freighted with risk, but also promise.

Pisano casts the scene moments after the birth; both Elizabeth and the child have survived and are doing well. Now she can rest, her work completed, the immediate danger from the childbirth now over. One of the attendants holds the baby while another holds a towel. They are preparing for his bath — a fitting first experience for someone whose entire ministry will have to do with cleansing, though for him cleansing of the outside will come in symbolic representation of the cleansing within. The scene is calm, a moment frozen for us in gilded bronze.

Now the time came for Elizabeth to give birth.

A s Tintoretto (1518-1594, Italy) portrays the scene, everything is chaos and movement. The baby's bath is over, and other attendants have arrived to assist in his care and in the care of his mother. Perhaps for just this once he is discretely given a white undergarment.

(Portrayals of the child John often depict him naked or clothed already in camel's hair robes; he is usually identifiable by his cross-topped staff — another anachronism that serves emblematic rather than historical truth.) There are limits to the discretion one might expect at such a moment, and one of the ladies has bared her own breast to nurse the child. By giving the woman darker hair,

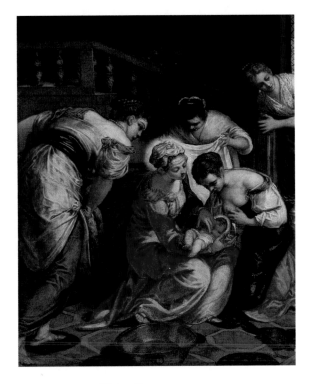

Tintoretto
The Birth of John the Baptist (Detail)
c. 1554 | oil on canvas | 181 x 266 cm
The Hermitage | St. Petersburg

Tintoretto has indicated that she is younger; her rather full breasts suggest that she may have a child of her own, but that she has come ready to play the wet-nurse because of Elizabeth's advanced age.

49

Tintoretto
The Birth of John the Baptist (Detail)
c. 1554 | oil on canvas | 181 x 266 cm
The Hermitage | St. Petersburg

On the right, Zechariah has come upon the scene unexpectedly, and has turned his eyes heavenward, perhaps in prayer, more likely in embarrassment at the sight of the wet-nurse's exposed breast.

A child watches from the stairs. Curiously, a chicken and a puppy tussle over scraps in the center foreground.

Clearly frail now, and exhausted from the effort and danger of the birth, Elizabeth watches from the bed. One of the women attends to her needs; another brings cloths to assist the wet-nurse.

One has the impression that Elizabeth must be well loved now. The women in the community have pitched in to assist. The old shame of rejection has been reversed. Like her younger cousin, Elizabeth is literally blessed among women.

Now the time came for **Elizabeth** to give birth.

All of this is in preparation for the birth of the Christ, but John's birth is no less a work of grace, and in its own way it also speaks to us no less forcefully of the hand of God. Everything about this hints of the miraculous — Zechariah's encounter with an angel in the temple, the instructions about the name, the fact that the old man has been struck mute, the pregnancy itself, then the leaping of the unborn Baptist in his mother's womb.

What Elizabeth cannot know is that later generations will read in her story a kind of literary foregrounding for the more miraculous birth of the Christ-child, just as the preaching of the Baptist will prepare the way for Jesus, and John's untimely death will cast its long shadow over the narrative and set the psychological stage for the crucifixion of the Christ that will follow.

Now the time came for **Elizabeth** to give birth.

His Name is John

Jacopo Pontormo
The Birth of John the Baptist
1526 | oil | 54 cm diameter
Galleria Uffizi | Florence

B y watching carefully, Italian artist Jacopo Pontormo (1494-
1557) has managed to capture one of the moments of high
drama in the story — the naming of the child. It is eight days
after the child's birth, and Elizabeth has fully recovered. One has the
sense that this is a solemn moment, a ceremony of great importance,
and Zechariah, Elizabeth, and the infant Baptist have all donned their
haloes in recognition. Though he is often described as the

quintessential Mannerist, Pontormo has abandoned the exuberant colors and extravagant monumental figures of his typical Mannerism, electing instead to paint the scene in muted pinks and somber browns.

Custom dictates that the child be named after his father, or perhaps a respected relative, but Zechariah will disregard the pull of tradition and the push of family and friends: the boy's name will be John.

Zechariah is an old man here — as in the biblical story — and Pontormo has painted him thin and frail; he no doubt addresses his questioners with an old man's quiet resolve.

The quiet of the image belies what must have been an anguishing decision; it does not take much imagination to empathize with an old man who has longed all his life for a son, someone to carry on his name, but Zechariah is a righteous man and he makes good on the instructions of the angel. To make sure there will be no misunderstanding, he asks for a writing tablet: "His name is John," he writes. There. It is done. The decision is made. The die is cast.

This decision has not come easily, but it is clear that Zechariah's long inner battle has been relegated to the distant past. The casual way he crosses his legs to hold the writing tablet on one knee indicates that he has no more of the old fight in him, and the declaration that the boy will be named John has become a settled conviction. In a moment, he will offer his own prophecy to echo that of the angel.

His boy will be what the angel had said:

> And you, child,
> will be called the prophet of the Most High;
> for you will go before the Lord to prepare his ways,
> to give knowledge of salvation to his people
> by the forgiveness of their sins.
> By the tender mercy of our God,
> the dawn from on high will break upon us,
> to give light to those who sit in darkness
> and in the shadow of death,
> to guide our feet into the way of peace.

All that remains now is to wait.

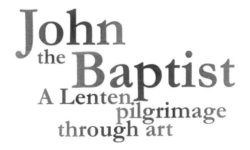

John the Baptist
A Lenten pilgrimage through art

John
the
Baptist
A Lenten
pilgrimage
through art

Mary and Elizabeth:
A Lenten Reflection

In these images of Mary and Elizabeth we see already the threads that interweave John's story with that of Jesus. The two stories unfold brightly, tapestries with dazzling weft, spectacular in their implications, but woven against dark warps, the vertical lines on the loom that hold the weft in place.

Thus these stories of promised redemption are told against a dark under-weaving of difficulty and doubt, and even tragedy. There are hints of the difficulty everywhere, showing through the brightness the way the basic warp threads of a thick cloth show through the weft threads that rest on top. Elizabeth's long years of childlessness, the disgrace; then the dangerous pregnancy late in life; the challenges Mary will face: the disparaging rumors among the neighbors, the public disgrace of her family and the family of her fiancé. Then, in a final twist of Providence, all of it followed in time by the dark fates of these two infants. Who knows which of these two mothers will suffer the greater loss — Elizabeth who did not live to see the promise of her husband's prophecy fulfilled, or Mary who was with her son at the very end?

None of that is set aside here, and instead in these images we learn that even the darker threads have their place within the overall pattern that the Weaver has created. The dark under-weave of the warp tells us that the work of God is not always safe, and that it sometimes asks us to summon the strength to suffer supreme sacrifices. It would be more than anyone could bear, except for this: the warp that forms the underlying patterns is also the work of a creative and redemptive God, who weaves the weft over top the warp to make these tapestries of extraordinary beauty and depth.

If these stories teach us anything, it is this: the bright threads of the over-weave may give the tapestries of life their beauty, but it is the dark threads of the under-weave that give them their depth.

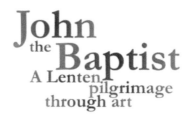

John
the Baptist
A Lenten pilgrimage
through art

The child grew
and became
strong in spirit.
strong in spirit.
strong in spirit.

John
the Baptist
A Lenten pilgrimage through art

The Childhood of the Baptist

William-Adolphe Bougeureau
Young John the Baptist
1887

The biblical record gives no evidence that John and Jesus ever saw each other growing up, though that is not impossible. St Matthew suggests that Jesus was whisked away to safety during the events known as the Massacre of the Innocents. There is an apocryphal story that they met in the desert on the return of the Holy Family, a story that has often been exploited in the artistic tradition. Thus the child John is shown in playful interaction with the child Christ.

In a childhood portrait by William-Adolphe Bouguereau (1825-1905), John appears an innocent, looking heavenward. Even at this young age, he has been given his first and most enduring emblem — a shirt of hair-cloth.

So even as a child John is burdened with a message. In an unfinished tondo *bas relief* by Michelangelo (1475-1564), he attempts to deliver his message to the infant Jesus. Named after the family of Taddeo Taddei, the piece was created around 1504, while Michelangelo was also working on the *David*. Because the tondo was never completed, art historians have examined it closely for clues about the sculptor's use of his tools and habits of work. Even unfinished, the *Taddei Madonna* creates a strong visual impression as the rough figures seem to move rapidly across the chiseled face of the stone.

There is a deep human connectedness in this piece. On the left, identified by the baptismal cup tied to his waist, John chases the Christ child, offering him a gift of a bird. No doubt the viewer is expected to interpret the bird as an emblem of the Holy Spirit, and thus as a prefiguring of the ministry Jesus is to assume when the two have grown up. Jesus, reluctant, dives headlong into the protective arms of his mother. He is not yet ready. The day will come. Not yet.

The child grew
and became
strong in spirit.
strong in spirit.
strong in spirit.

He is less reluctant in *The Madonna of the Meadow,* by Italian artist Raphael (1483-1520). The artist has caught Mary, Jesus, and John on an outing in the Florentine countryside. No doubt Joseph, Elizabeth, and Zechariah are nearby, keeping watch.

The comfortable triangular grouping creates a strong sense of balance and harmony, a harmony increased by the gentleness of the distant background and the stillness of the lake. Mary looks particularly graceful here as she steadies the infant Christ; her features are delicate and balanced, her expression at ease. It is the poise of a holy woman at peace with the world.

What is noteworthy here is that John has picked up another of the emblems that will distinguish him throughout the remaining history of Christian art — he holds a reed staff with a small cross at the top. We will see this emblem repeatedly in the portrayals of John that follow. In time it will come to carry a narrow banner with the words ECCE AGNUS DEI — *Behold the Lamb of God* — fluttering in the breeze. But that is in the distant future, and the two boys have no idea what the emblems mean. For now they play, as children will, safe within Mary's sheltering gaze, indifferent to the implications of the staff and the cross.

Abbott Anderson Thayer
A Virgin
1892-1893 | oil on canvas
90.4 in x 71.8 in
Freer Gallery of Art | Washington

John
the Baptist
A Lenten pilgrimage through art

...and he was
in the
wilderness
until the day
he appeared
publicly
to Israel.

. . . . and he was
in the
wilderness
until the day
he appeared
publicly
to Israel.

The Youth in the Wilderness

Thus far Luke's account has been slow and detailed, a meandering journey covering only a few brief encounters spread out over less than a year. Suddenly the language turns quick — thirty years in a single verse. It is so quick it leaves us breathless:

> The child grew and became strong in spirit, and he was in the wilderness until the day he appeared publicly to Israel.

What happened out there, anyway? The Bible does not tell us, an oversight that has left this period of John's life open to intense scholarly and devotional speculation. The artists, who were forced to rely entirely on their imaginations, seem to have seized the moment to portray in John a man with an ideal character even in youth. The trick lies in the classical identification of physical form with spiritual beauty. John must have been a beautiful boy, so the reasoning goes, and so they painted beautiful boys.

Andrea del Sarto
John the Baptist
1528 | oil on wood | 94 x 68 cm
Gallaria Palatina | Florence

One of the most beautiful is by Andrea del Sarto (1483-1530, Italy), painted in 1528, just two years before the artist's death. The infant Baptist has grown into a youth. Notice that he has acquired another of his emblems — the red mantle, symbol of the martyr. The other emblems seem to have been arranged in a kind of studio pose: he holds the bowl in his right hand, and the shirt of haircloth has been thrown back to reveal a strong, clean torso. The cross has been strategically placed in the lower right.

As beautiful as this boy is, there is a kind of sadness in those eyes. Can he have had an inkling of what lies ahead for him, and for his young cousin? He is old beyond his years.

John
the Baptist
A Lenten pilgrimage
through art

...and he was in the wilderness until the day he appeared publicly to Israel.

Caravaggio (1573-1610, Italy) painted several variations on this theme. This one, painted about 1603, shows John as a boy of maybe fourteen, thin and wiry. He appears to have been awakened in the night, and Caravaggio catches him balancing himself as he sits up. His hair is disheveled, and he is entangled in his bedclothes. He has been using the red robe as a blanket against the cold desert night.

His baptismal cup rests beside him; he has brought it along from the *Taddei Madonna*. In the slow assembly of emblems he is growing closer to the full identity which will mark his role in the world. The dove is gone for now; it will return to complete the ensemble when John has been made fully ready to respond to his call, and when Jesus appears on the scene for baptism. For now, we wait.

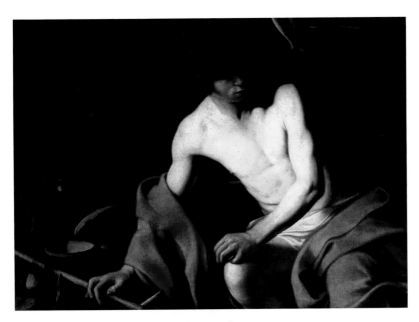

Caravaggio
St John the Baptist
1603-04 | oil on canvas | 94 x 131 cm
Galleria Nazionale d'Arte Antica | Rome

But waiting is difficult, especially for a young man, and no doubt John has been pondering the meaning of these emblems he has been carrying around. They will ask something of him. He is being equipped, but for what?

John has been given a staff with a cross, a bowl, a hair shirt, and a mantle of deep blood red. He is drawn inexplicably to the desert, the wildness of life on the edge, life unconfused by the seductions of the city. He feels a strong affinity for sheep, which somehow enter his life at unexpected moments, speak to him of something sacred, something to do with his very identity. How is he to go about finding the common thread that connects these disparate items into a coherent response to the call of God?

Georges de La Tour
St John the Baptist in the Desert
c. 1650 | oil on canvas | 101 x 81 cm
Conseil général de la Moselle

These are disturbing questions, as we see in the portrayal by Georges de la Tour (1593-1662, France). The disturbances in the night have continued. Like the young prophet Samuel, John has been startled awake. He is unaware of where or who he is.

Here de la Tour, a master of single source illumination, has captured the youthful Baptist in the eerie moonlight of the desert. As he holds the staff with its cross in his left hand he struggles to grasp its meaning, connecting it for the first time, perhaps, with the lamb that he feeds from his baptismal bowl. He has carried the staff since he was a child in Raphael's *Madonna of the Meadow*. Is it a dream or a nightmare? Is it a high and holy calling? Will it be dangerous? Will he be equal to the demands it may make upon him? It is significant that as he ponders these questions, he shares his concern and consternation with the

Agnus Dei whose way he has come to prepare.

De la Tour's painting might well have been entitled, *The Dark Night of the Soul.* Its subject is, literally, John of the cross.

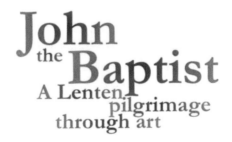

It is lighter here, in another of Caravaggio's portrayals of this scene. Dawn has come. John has been up all night, unable to sleep, and the struggle with the staff has been consuming. Caravaggio has captured in John's deeply furrowed brow the struggle of the youth pondering the fully grown man he is to become, not yet fully understanding what manhood is about, what it will ask of him, whether he will have the internal clarity or courage to follow through on whatever task God may have set for him. The muscles of his jaw are set, and his mouth is fixed into a permanent, brooding frown.

He has discovered the meaning of the baptismal bowl, and it is troubling.

He is to call Israel back to God.

Certainly he does not have the political stature. He is the son of a priest, but is certainly not a prophet. He is just a youth, he knows no one, he has no life in the city, he is an outsider, he is a wild boy in the desert. Who is he to assume such a role?

Equally puzzling, perhaps most puzzling of all, is the meaning of the staff with its small cross. Perhaps it is a clue to the content of his message, but it is an unclear clue. Why is God not more clear? He struggles to discover the Will of God, but he takes no delight in the struggle.

...and he was in the wilderness until the day he appeared publicly to Israel.

Antonio d'Enrico
St John the Baptist
C 1627-1629 | oil on canvas
Philbrook Museum | Tulsa

In this portrait, Italian artist Antonio d'Enrico (1575/80-1635) tells us of a further, critical step in John's discovery of his call: the lamb.

The internal situation has reached its apex. Every muscle is taught; the grip on the staff is white-knuckled like his grip on his calling. The painting sweeps us diagonally upward from the lamb in the lower left to the object of John's imploring gaze in the upper right, outside of the frame of the painting, probably outside the frame of the physical world as well. John has discovered the last critical clue in the emblem of the sheep. He gestures downward, identifying the lamb, and his upward gaze seeks final confirmation. The Kingdom cannot come until the Lamb of God has been revealed to the world. This is how God will call Israel back to God's self.

The lamb, then, provides the meaning of the staff. Before we meet him again John will have printed out the words that will add to his ministry its requisite grace if it is to be truly the work of a holy man:

Ecce Agnus Dei
Behold the Lamb of God.

...and he was
in the
wilderness
until the day
he appeared
publicly
to Israel.

On Finding God in the Desert:
A Lenten Reflection

We have traced John's developing identity through the emblems by which the artistic tradition has interpreted his work. Not all of the emblems would make sense to the boy; he must await the clarity that comes with manhood, and with his own encounter with God. John must discover who he is by drawing these disparate, disconnected gifts together, understanding that the gifts God has given him may themselves be the voice by which God tells him who he is and what he is to do.

At times the Will of God comes clear to us in this same way. We are equipped with an apparently disconnected array of gifts, or signals that come to us without context, and so we must puzzle and pray and ponder what they mean. It can be disorienting, like being startled awake from a sound sleep and not being certain where or who we are. So we are not so different from John after all.

It is significant that for John the call happens in the desert. He is not alone in this regard. Moses learned the name of God in the wilderness, just as he learned the will of God — chiseled on the tablets of the Decalogue — in the isolation of Mt. Sinai.

Several of John's forerunners among the prophets heard the prophetic call of God in the desert. Nor is John the last to experience the call of God in the desert. Jesus will spend his forty days in the wilderness, wrestling with, sorting out, his call. In the 4th and 5th Centuries, a veritable flood of monks and anchorites will seek refuge in the desert from the conflicts and confusions of the life in the city. The Christian tradition is graced with wonderful stories of the Desert Fathers and, we are learning, Mothers as well. Monasteries that grew up out of the stone outcroppings more than fifteen hundred years ago are still with us today — stone symbols of a severe and simple spirituality.

Desert spirituality is with us in other ways as well, most especially in the withdrawals and contemplations that comprise the observance of Lent, as we prepare ourselves, like John, for the holy work of the Kingdom of God.

What is it about the desert that creates this powerful magnetic pull on the spiritually minded? Why subject oneself to the loneliness, the deprivations, difficulties, and dangers? What is it about the desert that can turn the son of a priest into a radical preacher of repentance in the wilderness who passes judgment on the whole world he has left behind?

Certainly there is the stillness. Sometimes we must leave behind the cacophony — the clatter and clamor — and quiet our hearts as we seek the still small voice in which God so often seems to speak.

And there is the immensity. The night sky is scattered with stars, flung there by the hand of God. The canopy of constellations is a chancel choir that in its silence sings to us of the immensity of God and the smallness and fragility of the human presence in God's enormous universe. The music of the spheres puts us in our place.

But most of all there are the hardships, which serve as constant reminders of our creatureliness — our utter dependence on God for our very breath.

In this way the wilderness itself is turned into an emblem, a symbolic reminder that even when we are most desolate, still God is there, comforting us and calling to us in our despair.

Those who embark on pilgrimages often report that the transforming moments come, not when they reach the famous shrines in the company of other pilgrims, but when they find themselves alone in the Company of the Creator.

The voice of
one crying out
in the wilderness
"Make straight
the way
of the Lord!"

The voice of
one crying out
in the wilderness
"Make straight
the way
of the Lord!"

The Eschatological Prophet

Giovanni Baciccio
The Preaching of St John the Baptist
c. 1690 | oil on canvas | 181 x 172 cm
The Louvre | Paris

In this piece by Italian artist Giovanni Baciccio (1639-1709), John
has at last found his voice. The banner tells the tale: *Ecce agnus Dei
— Behold the Lamb of God.* John's finger is raised in oratory. No
doubt he is teaching about the ethical and religious implications of the
coming Kingdom. The crowds are already large here — women, men,
children. In the lower right a woman turns, distracted from her breast-
feeding by the power of John's preaching. A hand is raised within the
crowd, and someone else lurches back, startled, as a man on a white
horse gallops into the scene. The crowds are in turmoil.

Why have they come? John has all of the trappings of a prophet here, and a prophet is what they have been waiting for. He is dressed like Elijah. He proclaims the nearness of the Kingdom of God. And he makes nearly impossible demands, unheard of demands. He tells them that even from Jews — already part of the Chosen People — God requires something more: repentance and a change of life, all of it symbolized by the rite of baptism.

It is springtime in this picture. Baciccio is telling us indirectly that even in the desert there are well-springs of new life.

The voice of
one crying out
in the wilderness
"Make straight
the way
of the Lord!"

Pieter Breughel the Elder
The Preaching of John the Baptist
1566 | oil on canvas | 95 x 161 cm
Museum of Fine Arts | Budapest

E very artist who has painted John has had to wrestle with the
temptation to focus on the oddities--the wild eyes, the peculiar
dress, the emblems, the finger raised in accusation or oratory.
This is one temptation that, remarkably, Pieter Breughel the Elder
(1520-1569, Netherlands) has managed to resist. If it weren't for the
title, we would not know that this is "The preaching of John the
Baptist," and we would suppose instead that it is a simple gathering of
peasants from the Low Countries, come out to the forest perhaps to
celebrate an impromptu festival.

The scene is all trees and heads, and the viewer literally has to search
for the Baptist in the crowd. Some children have perched in the trees,
listening. In the background: the river, a tell-tale giveaway. In the right

87

foreground, a pair of latecomers confer. Someone is asking questions, investigating.

In the center, apparently dressed in his hair shirt, the Baptist preaches. Even though the crowd is still, we can barely hear him. He is completely swallowed up in the crowd. But perhaps Breughel intends another message here: John is lost behind the message. In a sense, he is already on the decline. All that matters now is the message itself.

The voice of one crying out in the wilderness "Make straight the way of the Lord!"

"Thou art my beloved Son. In thee I am well pleased."

"Thou art my beloved Son. In thee I am well pleased."

The Baptism of Jesus

A nd then, just as John's ministry gains momentum, there is a pause. The storyline turns mystical, rather than political or even religious. John stops cold in his remonstrations and his harangues to perform his rite of Baptism upon the One whose way he has come to prepare.

By all accounts, the baptism of Jesus is one of the seminal moments of John's career, a moment pregnant with theological meaning. There is something about the Baptism that turns a corner for Jesus as well. His face is grave. Perhaps it is the final confirmation of his call to do — to *be* — the Kingdom John has been proclaiming. Perhaps it is in his realization that the designation *Beloved Son* will be freighted with danger, recalling the words by which the Bible describes Abraham's sacrifice of his own beloved son Isaac.

In another watercolor, James Tissot depicts the scene as a Trinitarian affirmation. The dove of the Holy Spirit has settled on Jesus' shoulder, and a Presence of some sort descends upon his head.

By all accounts, the baptism of Jesus is one of the seminal moments of John's career, a moment pregnant with theological meaning. There is something about the Baptism that turns a corner for Jesus as well. His face is grave. Perhaps it is the final confirmation of his call to do—to *be*—the Kingdom John has been proclaiming. Perhaps it is in his realization that the designation *Beloved Son* will be freighted with danger, recalling the words by which the Bible describes Abraham's sacrifice of his own beloved son Isaac.

In another watercolor, James Tissot depicts the scene as a Trinitarian affirmation. The dove of the Holy Spirit has settled on Jesus' shoulder, and a Presence of some sort descends upon his head.

The crowds are here to watch and to assist. Two of the onlookers prepare white robes for Jesus for when this symbolic moment is completed. Others, more reticent, peer from the rushes at the water's edge.

John
the Baptist
A Lenten
pilgrimage
through art

"Thou art my beloved Son. In thee I am well pleased."

The crowds have reason to be reticent. There is something going on here, something of the heavens, and they do not entirely understand what it is. In this finely crafted tapestry by JOHN NAVA (1947-, American) they have withdrawn completely, and the emblems have been set aside. Time stops. The artist has given us just these two men, frozen in time, captured in the quiet rippling of the cloth. Jesus kneels in the water. The world is transformed in the stillness. It is a holy moment, a moment out of time. Yet there is action here, too: the weave of the cloth reflects the flowing water of the Jordan, rivering through the scene. At points we have the impression that Jesus and John have become one with the river.

On one level this is a monumental project—the banner into which the scene is woven is nearly forty-eight feet tall; it dominates a chapel in the Cathedral of the Angels in Los Angeles. The figures are larger than life.

On another level, one is struck, not by the power of the figures, but by their shared humility. Jesus has appeared on the edge of the Jordan and requested baptism. John has demurred:

> "I need to be baptized by you, and do you come to me?"

Jesus, in turn, submits himself to John's ministry:

> "Let it be so now; for thus it is fitting for us to fulfill all righteousness."

Theologians speculate that this is a crisis moment for Jesus. Soon we will find him in the desert, experiencing his own Dark Night of the Soul. The stress will be so great that he will be unable to eat. In preparation, he kneels before the Baptist, submitting himself symbolically and sacramentally to the will of God.

From this time forward, John's ministry will be on the descent, and Jesus' will be on the rise. Even so, St Mark tells us that even after the Temptation in the Wilderness, Jesus will wait until John has been "handed over." Jesus, Beloved Son, Messiah designate, will still defer to John.

"Thou art my beloved Son. In thee I am well pleased."

"I am not the Christ."
"I am not."
"NO!"

John and the Jewish Authorities

The time out of time has been left behind, and John resumes his ministry. His zeal has now caught the attention of the authorities. Seldom in the history of the world has there been someone with this much charismatic power. The authorities are not stupid. They realize well enough that an eschatological prophet can spell serious trouble for the status quo. A man on fire in the wilderness is a dangerous thing.

They take no chances. This could have something to do with revolt, and the whole desert thing smacks of secrecy. And whatever else, the fact that he does his work in the desert suggests an implicit opposition to the cities, to the temple, to the very work that they do in the maintenance of their religion. At best, John seems to be dismissing them as irrelevant; at worse he could be accusing them of outright fraud in the name of God. If they fail to pay attention, their world could come tumbling down on top of them, temple and all.

James Tissot
St John the Baptist and the Pharisees
1886-1894 | opaque watercolor over graphite on gray woven paper
6 3/16 x 9 1/16 in | Brooklyn Museum of Art

In this watercolor by James Tissot, they send investigators out to try and get a finger on what the man is up to, what he is planning. Their backs are to us and we cannot hear their questions. Even so, we can gather critical information from the increasing brevity of John's answers:

"I am not the Christ."
"I am not."
"No."

He is growing impatient. His final reply is cryptic and an affront to his questioners: "I baptize with water; but among you stands one whom you do not know, even he who comes after me, the thong of whose sandal I am not worthy to untie."

The Messiah, the One whose way John has come to prepare, is someone they — the official representatives of the Jewish religion — simply do not know, even though he stands among them, in their very midst! John is remembering stories his father told him about the Florentine dignitaries in the nave of Ghirlandaio's painting of the visit from the angel Gabriel: these people are in the presence of holiness and they do not know enough to take off their shoes.

What makes the exchange explosive is the fact that this comes as a challenge to their piety and their competence, and it is delivered in public, with the whole mass of the people looking on. The tension in the story mounts. They are not finished with John, not by a long shot.

Mattia Preti
St John the Baptist Preaching
c. 1665 | oil on canvas | 85 1/2 x 67 in
Fine Arts Museum | San Francisco

But John is not finished with them, either. In a portrayal by Mattia Preti (1613-1699, Italy) he has become ferocious:

"You brood of vipers! Who warned you to flee from the wrath to come? ... Even now the axe is laid to the root of the trees; every tree therefore that does not bear good fruit is cut down and thrown into the fire."

His banner is larger here, more prominent, his face more intense, his finger more accusatory; the paint itself seems to boil in the heat of it.

He now sweeps across the theological landscape like a force of nature, echoing the thunderclouds that form the backdrop of the painting. The intensity of the call has taken its toll on his appearance, and the changes are striking: his beard has grown out, and his hair — once worn long after the fashion of aristocratic Florence — has grown unkempt and disheveled. He has engaged his mission and nothing else is important to him. The force of his prophetic call has transformed him into a wild man. He is all fire and snakes. He has had no choice in the matter. He is no longer a man with a mission, but the mission itself is all that is left. His call has engulfed him, swallowed him whole. He has become a burning bush.

The wildness is not without theological significance of its own. His hair-shirt recalls the prophet Elijah, with his thundering denunciations. Other emblems are also here — John has discovered their significance. The sheep, the staff and its ribbon announce the arrival of *ho erchomenos*, the Coming One, the Lamb of God who will take away the sin of the world.

John goes about his work with a vengeance becoming of an eschatological prophet. He is Elijah, delivering his message in a thundering jeremiad:

"Repent, for the Kingdom of God is at hand."

Thus he fulfills Malachi's prophecy and the prediction of his father:

"Behold, I will send you Elijah the prophet before the great and terrible day of the LORD comes. And he will turn the hearts of fathers to their children and the hearts of children to their fathers, lest I come and smite the land with a curse."

If ever there was a hell-fire and brimstone preacher, it is John. He is fierce for the Kingdom. He spares no one. It is not enough to engage in the practice of religion, he thunders. The Kingdom demands that we become so enflamed with the call of God that we too are totally engulfed, swallowed whole.

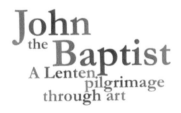

John
the Baptist
A Lenten
pilgrimage
through art

Mattia Preti
The Baptist Before Herod
1665
Oil on Canvas
90 x 190 cm
New York: Private Collection

In another piece — also by Mattia Preti — John decides to set fire to Herod's obscene pretentions. He has condemned commoner and clergy; in this piece he castigates king and court. To be sure, Herod was never a king, but only a tetrarch with monarchical pretensions, a tetrarch who lived in his father's shadow. The operative word here is *pretensions*; such a man will trample under foot anyone he suspects might get in his way.

Perhaps that is why Preti's painting is so startling: On the one hand, he has captured the Baptist at a moment of wild-eyed courage. John's accusatory finger leaves no doubt about what he thinks of Herod and his illicit dalliances with his brother's wife, Herodias. John has become a wild man; he finally speaks truth to power:

"It is not right for you to have your brother's wife."

It is a public affront, and thus a gauntlet thrown down, but it is what we have come to expect from a man like John. He holds nothing back.

Still, the look on Herod's face leaves the viewer puzzled. In other circumstances what we would expect from a man like Herod would be seething rage. Here he rests his chin upon his hand, and it appears at first that he is bored. But within the artistic tradition, a chin resting on a hand connotes deep, solitary  contemplation. Instead of lashing out, Herod has drawn back within himself. Because he is a superstitious man, we are allowed to infer that the external calm masks a deep inner struggle.

Why this struggle? Perhaps he is aware that John's condemnation is shared by both the common people and the religious establishment. Could it be that John is a prophet, and that he, Herod, has reason to fear the wrath of God as well?

And so Herod hesitates.

Then, as suddenly as he had arrived, John turns and leaves the court, back to the wilderness from which he had come, back to resume his primary work.

But Herod the ruler,
who had been rebuked by John
because of Herodias
His brother's wife,
And because of all the evil things
Herod had done.
added to them all by
shutting John in prison.

John
the Baptist
A Lenten pilgrimage through art

The Incarceration of John

It cannot end that easily. Herod is a superstitious and petty man, and despite the possibility that John may be a prophet, he knows the man has to be silenced. As John's preaching becomes more strident, the crowds are growing larger and more restive. The situation is growing volatile.

But there are positive signs in the way the Bible tells the story. Herod wants John silenced, but he has no designs on the Baptist's life. That distinction falls to his wife, Herodias, who "has a grudge against John and wants him dead." St Mark tells us that Herod hears John gladly enough, and even that he keeps him safe from Herodias' criminal machinations.

And so Herod has John arrested.

But **Herod the ruler**,
who had been **rebuked by John**
because **of Herodias**
His brother's wife,
And because of **all the evil things**
Herod had done.
added to them all by
shutting **John** in prison.

Andrea Pisano
The Incarceration of St John
1330-1336 | bronze bas relief | 49.7 x 43.2 cm
The Baptistery of the Cathedral | Florence

To visualize the scene, we turn to another of Andrea Pisano's *bas relief* panels on the doors of the Baptistery of the Florence Cathedral. True to his carefully controlled artistic sensibilities and the requirements of his bronze medium, Pisano has given us a simple image, spare of details. We have the jailor, leading the way, John himself, and the arresting soldiers. One of the soldiers, ominously, carries a sword. The prison is represented by a simple grille.

In another part of the palace the plot thickens as tension builds between Herod and his conniving hellcat of a wife. Along with John and his many followers, we hold our breath.

But Herod the ruler,
who had been rebuked by John
because of Herodias
His brother's wife,
And because of all the evil things
Herod had done.
added to them all by
shutting John in prison.

On the Perplexity of John in Prison: A Lenten Reflection

It is almost impossible to imagine the distress John is now under. For such a man, the agony of imprisonment is not in being confined so much as it is in being silenced. The Baptist has become a burning bush behind bars.

Even so, it does not take much imagination to envision John solitary and smoldering within his prison cell. He had expected a Messiah who was like himself, only more so. Remember his preaching?

> "You brood of vipers! Who warned you to flee from the wrath to come? Bear fruits that befit repentance, and do not begin to say to yourselves, 'We have Abraham as our father'; for I tell you, God is able from these stones to raise up children to Abraham. Even now the axe is laid to the root of the trees; every tree therefore that does not bear good fruit is cut down and thrown into the fire."

> "I baptize you with water; but he who is mightier than I is coming, the thong of whose sandals I am not worthy to untie; he will baptize you with the Holy Spirit and with fire. His winnowing fork is in his hand, to clear his threshing floor, and to gather the wheat into his granary, but the chaff he will burn with unquenchable fire."

The message throbs with apocalyptic images, images of judgment and tribulation, wailing, and the gnashing of teeth.

And yet, when Jesus appears, he seems very much unlike John. John calls people to desert spirituality; Jesus meets people where they live. John harangues; Jesus tells stories. John is an ascetic; he avoided even the best of them. Jesus appears to have partied with the worst of them. The Bridegroom whose way John has come to prepare seems to celebrate life with a moveable feast; everywhere he goes he flings the doors wide open and extends the invitation to anyone who will come!

It is not difficult to imagine John imagining that Jesus has lost his way. The dissonance is so great that he finally sends someone to Jesus to check: "Are you He Who is to Come, or should I be looking for another?" We would have to be deaf to miss the anguish in John's question. "Have I done all of this in vain?"

Jesus' response to John is telling:

> "Go and tell John what you hear and see: the blind receive their sight and the lame walk, lepers are cleansed and the deaf hear, and the dead are raised up, and the poor have good news preached to them."

Jesus' words here contain an allusion to a famous passage in the book of Isaiah, describing what came to be understood as the ultimate theme of the Messianic Age — *Shalom.* Jesus seems to be saying, "It is not enough to make them holy; we must also make them whole." John's truth, while true, is not the Whole Truth. It takes the ministry of Jesus for that.

So Jesus and John are unalike, and John does not fully understand this difference. How can the same God be at work in men of such totally different temperaments, with such totally different views of redemption?

In a sense, John's perplexity is ours as well: How can God call us to perform a task in the world, and then sit by and watch as our work seems to come completely to naught? The question reminds us that the workings of the Kingdom are mysterious, beyond our ability to understand. God's ways are not our ways. We are asked to be faithful to the light that we have, and to trust that even in our perplexities and disappointments — even in our deserts and our prison cells, even on our sickbeds — God's work of redemption is more sweeping and more stunning than we are able to imagine.

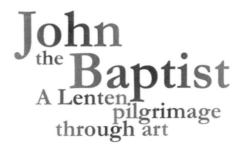

John
the Baptist
A Lenten pilgrimage through art

And immediately
the king sent
a soldier of the guard
and gave orders
to bring
his head.

The Death of a Prophet

The beheading of John the Baptist is one of the most frequently painted of the biblical scenes. There are several suggestions about why this is so, but I think the most likely is that the tensions within the story present significant artistic challenges, and therefore also the chance for the artists to display their skills.

Bernardino Luini
Salome Receiving the Head of John the Baptist
1527 | oil on panel | 24 ½ x 20 ¼ in
Museum of Fine Arts | Boston

In the artist's imaginations, what we have here is a presumably lovely young woman depicted perpetrating an absolutely barbarous act. The crucial issue has to do with the girl's face: is she horrified? Or is she calm, as here, in this famous piece by Bernardino Luini (c. 1440-1532, Italy)?

At first glance it would appear that she is handling the head herself, but closer inspection subverts that. The hand in the upper right is larger and differently colored than the hand that holds the platter, and it wears a different type of sleeve. Notice, too, that Salome's right arm has no muscle tension; she is not yet carrying the weight of what she has done. Her mind is elsewhere. Her face is turned away impassively; one wonders why she does not look at the monstrosity she has created. Here she appears completely detached. Perhaps in a moment the heavy weight of the head on the platter will impress upon her the gravity of the choices she has made.

And immediately
the king sent
a soldier of the guard
and gave orders
to bring
his head.

What will her face tell us then? Will she be defiant, or even triumphant? She has become a monster — will it show on her face? St Thomas Aquinas once said that the face is the mirror of the soul. As evil as she is, will she still be seductive, as she is here, in this cover shot for the Salomé album by the contemporary German metal-rock band, Xandria?

There is a calmness about this image, and yet there are tensions, too. Salomé appears to hide discreetly behind her veil, but from behind the veil her eyes are penetrating and direct. They are a nearly unearthly shade of green. Her face is flawless, her makeup impeccable. It is an intriguing image, I think. She is anything but shy or self-effacing. Does it tell us something important about the attractiveness in which Evil may come packaged?

And immediately
the king sent
a soldier of the guard
and gave orders
to bring
his head.

Left to right:

- Henri Regnault, 1890
- Jean Benner, 1899
- J. Romani, 1898
- Onorio Marinari, 2nd half, 17th Century
- Gustav Klimt, 1909

In this shocking portrait, 16th Century Italian artist Cesare da Sesto (1477-1523) has given us an impish, self-possessed Salomé. She turns her head coyly to one side, almost winking off canvas at the viewer. With a delicate gesture, she indicates the head. The gesture and the sly smile tell us that she has no remorse (that will come later, perhaps); here she merely smiles, posing for the photograph. In context, the smile and the gesture are disquieting, and the executioner's face shows that he finds them disturbing. He stands there, holding the head, not over a platter, as we might expect, but over a bowl, indicating that the blood is still dripping. A hint of the blade glints in his other hand; he has only just now completed his work. Has she no idea what she has done?

How do we depict the head itself? Da Sesto has made it backdrop only. It's darker, impassive, a prop to offset the impishness of the girl. But is this all we can do? Is John still noble in death? Or was he frightened? Disheveled (as John is incessantly depicted in the iconography)? Does his head still wear its halo, or has the executioner's blade taken that off, too?

And immediately
the king sent
a soldier of the guard
and gave orders
to bring
his head.

Cesare da Sesto
Salomé with the Head of John the Baptist
c. 1515 | oil on panel | 80 x 136 inches
Kunsthistorisches Museum | Vienna

B ut let us return to the girl. When it comes to spiritual things, there remained a certain prudery in religious art, the fascination with the human body notwithstanding. (Caravaggio is the exception here.)

Perhaps this is understandable since the subject of religious art is generally not the physical world, but the spiritual. The result is that the depictions of Salomé and her dance are often understated, as they are here, in a depiction by 15th Century Italian artist, Fra Filippo Lippi (1406-1469).

Fra Filippo Lippi
The Feast of Herod
c. 1452-66 | Fresco
Prato Cathedral

It is a stylized depiction at best. The feast could have taken place in any Florentine palace, and the guests might have been any of the Medici family or their friends. Through a device called continuous representation, Fra Filippo has given us, in one scene, two moments in the story. On the left, Salomé performs in a flimsy organdy dress, while on the right she presents John's head to her mother. Everything appears frozen in a moment of time — or rather, two moments. The guests on the left are unaware of the horror on the right. They watch the girl, unaware of the drama that is unfolding before them in her dance.

And immediately
the king sent
a soldier of the guard
and gave orders
to bring
his head.

And immediately
the king sent
a soldier of the guard
and gave orders
to bring
his head.

It will take until the 20th Century before someone strikes out more boldly to depict the dance in its full sensuality. (This is closer, I think, to the depiction in our story — at least in Herod's imagination.)

This detail from a piece by German symbolist Franz von Stuck (1863-1928) has given us a Salomé who is completely without inhibitions. She is clearly no longer a girl, but is mature enough to capture the lurid imagination of her stepfather and his military officers. Unlike other portrayals of Salomé, the seduction here is not based on raw, sultry sensuality. This is no slow burn. Instead, it is the seductive abandon of youth and beauty. In the larger painting her breasts are exposed, but what is striking is the way she throws her head, which sends her headwear flying. Her eyes are not focused on anything in particular, but instead she is caught up completely within her own unrestrained freedom. Her dance is calculated to tell a man that there are no limits to what she might do — a perfect characterization, but with an outcome Herod could not have anticipated.

Franz von Stuck
Salomé (detail)
1906

Where is Herod? From the position of the figure, one might imagine that von Stuck has placed Herod precisely where the viewer stands. Directly in front, with full view. He watches. He hopes. He gives his imagination free reign to take him where it will. Whatever price she asks, Herod is willing to pay.

127

John
the Baptist
A Lenten pilgrimage through art

Caravaggio's own life was turbulent and disturbed, just as the scenes he paints are turbulent and disturbed. He seems to have preferred to paint violence. (He painted the beheading of John twice, and in the second — shown here — he signed his name in the Baptist's blood!) And yet — strikingly — his mastery over his medium is absolute and controlled. A man without perceptiveness could not have conceived of the infinitely subtle shading of composition or light to bring about these finely nuanced studies of emotion. And a man without patience could not have painted with such infinite, almost photographic, attention to detail.

The trap is set. The "king" makes his outrageous promise. The trap is sprung. The grisly outcome is recorded for us by Caravaggio (1573-1610, Italy). Twice.

The first depicts the moment of the beheading itself. The scene is set in the dark inner recesses of the prison, where the grisly murder is observed by two other prisoners looking through a grille (what must they be thinking?). A young girl and an old woman — doubtless serving women — stand ready to take the severed head and put it on the waiting platter. The painting is not mute. The older woman covers, not her eyes but her ears, a signal to the viewer to imagine the horrific sounds that must have accompanied this horrific event. A supervisor directs the action and the viewer's attention with a pointing finger. The blood flowing from St John's neck drips towards the bottom of the frame and in its red stream Caravaggio has signed his name.

Caravaggio
Salomé with the Head of John the Baptist
1610 | oil on canvas | 91 x 167 cm
National Gallery | London

In this second depiction, completed two years later in 1610 — the year of his own death — Caravaggio has captured the moment at which the head is delivered to Salomé on its required platter. Or perhaps the young woman is only a serving girl, and the presentation will come in a few moments. Caravaggio provides few clues other than the staging of the scene and the fact that the girl is modestly robed. The figures might well have been borrowed from the earlier piece depicted above, captured only moments later; the executioner has finished his grisly work, straightened up, and thrust the head onto the platter.

John's head is aged, its skin and hair reflecting the damaging effects of the sun and wind, and perhaps the psychological pressure the man had been under. As tradition has it, he was only about thirty years old, but here he looks considerably older. His mouth is open, as if he yet has something to say.

The two women refuse to look. The younger turns her head aside, and she holds the platter with the cloth of her scarf, as if touching the thing itself would somehow be defiling. The older woman has her eyes closed in disbelief; the sorrow on her face is profound.

In the end, it is the expression of disgust on the face of the executioner that captures the spirit of the painting. He has been required to do something which he no doubt finds morally repugnant; it is his job, but it is a distasteful, disturbing, despicable job. He plops the head down perfunctorily on the platter, to be done with it so he can get back to his quarters. He does not know and does not care about the revelers above, their revelry ruined, who await now the grisly outcome of the dance and the promise. As they wait, they ponder — no doubt — the consequences of the final withering of Herod's conscience and their complicit roles in the whole terrible debacle.

And immediately the king sent a soldier of the guard **and gave orders** to bring **his head.**

In most of these images, Herodias is strangely absent. Or is she? Is she not fully present in the outcome of the whole sordid affair? Consider this Baroque piece by Flemish master Peter Paul Rubens (1577-1640). The painting is entitled, *The Feast of Herod*, but the composition centers the viewer's attention on Herodias. Historically this is unlikely since the fortress in which John was beheaded had a separate dining hall for women, but what is that to art? Nevertheless it is fair to say that her presence loomed large here, even if she was in another room.

True to her character, Salomé has added another moment of drama to the tale: not only is the head brought in on its platter, but she has added a silver cover so she can serve it up like a fresh course at the dinner and catch her mother's reaction to that first glimpse.

Herodias is unimpressed. She might be a Victorian matron here — she is fair skinned and proper. She can barely suppress a smile. Above her shoulder, a sycophantic companion makes no effort to disguise her delight; she smiles sweetly, a foil for the bald man at the table, a bearded man (a soldier maybe?), what looks like a harmless monk, and a young boy in the foreground. There are others in the scene as well, but they are less visible in the turmoil; all but Herodias crowd in for a better look. At the back of the scene, barely visible, a servant goes about his work, continuing to bus dishes.

Notice that we have left behind the classical symmetry and formal composition in Fra Filippo's Florentine feast. The plot has progressed until, now in Baroque composition, everything is movement and tension.

What began as an evening birthday celebration has ended in turmoil — the feast has been turned to tumult. Only Herodias remains calm. She receives the head almost deferentially; the gestures of her hands are poised and delicate — "Oh my, what have we here?"

On the far right, identified by an ermine stole, Herod glares. It is difficult to see in this image, but with his left hand he grasps at the table linens — a not-so-transparent attempt to control his smoldering anger at what has happened.

Peter Paul Rubens
Sketch for The Feast of Herod
c. 1633-1638 | Pen and brown ink, black and red chalk | 27.2 × 47.2 cm
Museum of Art | Cleveland

His face is even more horrified in Rubens' preliminary sketch, but this is refined in the final painting. In the sketch, the characterization is carried by the king's royal frown; in the finished painting, it is carried by the grip on the tablecloth and the penetrating glare of the eyes.

And immediately
the king sent
a soldier of the guard
and gave orders
to bring
his head.

A nother take on Herod's reaction is captured for us in *bas relief* by Italian artist Donato di Niccolò Bardi (1386-1466). As Renaissance artists go, Donatello — as we know him — was early and influential. His studies in perspective paved the way for a much more realistic depiction of figures and their settings, and his detailed, relaxed portraiture anticipated the greater fluidity of movement characteristic of painting and sculpture in the High Renaissance in Italy. Commissioned in 1425 for one of the baptismal fonts of the Siena Cathedral, this *bas relief* embodies a famous early exploration of perspective.

Like Peter Paul Rubens, Donatello tells us that Herod was horrified, he and his guests alike — at the end of a sumptuous banquet, to be presented with something like that! One of the guests covers his eyes with his hand. In the lower left, two small children try to flee the scene, though one is turned back, no doubt driven by a kind of macabre voyeurism about the head, which appears to have been thrust unceremoniously onto Herod's lap. He recoils, his hands outstretched in a gesture of shock and dismay. He is appalled by what he has done.

John the Baptist
A Lenten pilgrimage through art

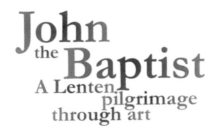

Ella Ferris Pell
Salomé
1890 | oil on canvas | 86.36 x 129.54 cm
Private collection

Who knows how long it will be before the players have packed their things and headed home? In the following piece by 19th Century American artist Ella Ferris Pell (1846-1922), Salomé pauses one last time before she leaves the hall.

She is clearly detached, or satisfied, her job of work completed for the evening. She holds the platter against a knee and looks off the canvas to her lower right. It is significant that she is swathed in a looming

darkness — a darkness to which she pays no attention whatever. She has focused instead on something off-scene, beneath her. She has paused one last time to survey the damage she has done. What does she see there? The carnage at the feast? Herod's face? John's head? His body? It little matters. Her project complete, she retreats into herself, not even bothering to compose her clothing. She is unaware that we are watching her. (Viewing this picture, one feels a little invasive.)

With the bare hint of an exposed breast the artist has reminded us that there are sensual nuances in the story after all, but so far as Herod is concerned they are set aside; the look on the girl's face borders on disdain. Nothing in the story suggests that she had brought the platter with her to the party (why would she do that?), and so we are left speculating: perhaps she has had it washed and is taking it home as a souvenir. She stands there alone, just as she will leave alone. There will be no illicit dalliance with her stepfather, not on this night. Likely never.

And immediately
the king sent
a soldier of the guard
and gave orders
to bring

his head.

Andrea Pisano
The Burial of John the Baptist
1330-1336 | bronze bas relief | 49.7 x 43.2 cm
The Baptistery of the Cathedral | Florence

S alomé is not the only one to note this scene with a sober air. The Bible tells us that John's disciples came and took the body and laid it in a tomb. Given the circumstances, it is an act of extraordinary courage.

Thirteen hundred years later and nearly 1600 miles away, they reenact the scene for us on another of Andrea Pisano's bronze tableaus on the Baptistery doors of the Florence cathedral. John's disciples have donned bronze robes for the occasion, softened by time now into a stately gray patina.

139

It is a fitting burial for a man many of them had no doubt hoped would be the Christ. Their faces are also gray, but that is only what one might expect; they're burying their dreams along with their teacher.

Five of them lean in close, tenderly lowering John's body into its coffin. Mercifully, they have somehow managed to recover his head, which they include in their holy work. On the near side of the coffin, two adjust the prophet's burial linens, while on the far side, two others keep solemn watch, as though the danger from Herod has not yet passed even after all these centuries. One is bearded and old, the other clean-shaven and young, an intergenerational reminder, perhaps, that "there went out to him all the country of Judea and the people of Jerusalem." But only perhaps. They have brought John to the Florence baptistery because it is a fitting resting place for a man who prophetically called the people to repentance, and who enabled that repentance through the sacrament of baptism. The sharp angles and gently rolling curves of the French quatrefoil surround suggest the stately cadences they will soon take up as they process into the baptistery to complete their sorrowful sacred task.

Gustave Moreau
The Apparition
1874-1876 | oil on canvas
142 cm x 103 cm
Musée Gustave Moreau | Paris

It remains for Gustave Moreau (1826-1898, France) to remind us that the story does not end with John's burial. He sets this painting — entitled, *The Apparition* — within Herod's tragically disturbed conscience.

Indeed, the subject of the painting is a sensitive reading of Mark 6:16. Rumors had been flying that another eschatological prophet had appeared in the Galilee. It was enough to drive Herod mad, yet as superstitious as he was, his remark reflects the astonishing perception that John and Jesus were about the same business: "But when Herod heard of it he said, 'John, whom I beheaded, has been raised.'" While in Mark's telling the statement comes early, in the absolute chronology it comes after the beheading, and it indicates that the event continued to trouble Herod, and not for the reasons we might suspect. The point for him wasn't that he had been bested by a girl in the presence of his friends, but that in the besting he had been manipulated into murdering a holy man. (Even the superstitious have reason to fear holiness.) Thus Moreau brings us finally to a moral conclusion: be sure our sins will find us out. At least in our minds, they will drip blood upon the floors of our inner palaces.

In an unexpected ironic reversal, it is the girl who points out the apparition to Herod. She is a study in her own right — the coy impishness has been stripped away, the satisfied disdain is gone, and the wild abandonment is replaced by horror. Moreau is telling us that Salomé has been brought to earth, her conscience also pricked — finally. Her mother wrings her hands.

In the personage of his head, John does indeed return to Herod, still the voice of moralist, prophet, and judge, symbolically reversing its role with the man on the throne. It is a Scarlet Letter of an accusation; it is Nathan accusing David for the murder of Uriah — "You are the man!" — and it tells Herod that not even murder will silence the voice of conscience: "*J'accuse!* — I accuse you! Salomé did not get you into this. Her dance merely brought out the perniciousness that was within you already."

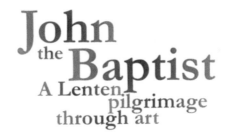

John
the Baptist
A Lenten pilgrimage
through art

And immediately
the king sent
a soldier of the guard
and gave orders
to bring
his head.

Purity of heart
is to
will
one
thing.

Purity of Heart is to Will One Thing:
A Lenten Reflection

In a short comment on the story of the Beheading of John, African theologian Victor Babajide Cole has said — rightly — that "we are in dire need of fearless modern prophets rather than praise singers who revel in high places, for sycophancy is rife."

Cole has reflected a common reading of this story, and he is right, of course. But let us look a little more deeply. It is common to see in this story the theme of the righteous man "speaking truth to power" and then suffering whatever consequences that might entail. When we view the story this way, the "power" we tend to envision is that of Herod — surely a tyrant and megalomaniac like his father. But the Bible does not say that Herod wants John dead; it says the opposite. Herod "fears John and keeps him safe," and when the trap is sprung, he is "exceedingly sorry." So the story poses a difficult problem: why could Herod not act on his better impulse and do the right thing? Clearly there was more to it than his lust for his step-daughter or his need to impress his friends.

In an extended discussion of Mark's overarching moral vision, Hispanic theologian Alberto de Mingo Kaminouchi has argued that Herod's problem is his political and social entanglements, which corrupt his vision and prevent him from making sound moral choices:

> Mark wants to show the reader how power works. Power can be imagined as the property of the powerful. It is normally accepted that some people, like the rulers, have power. The

vision presented by Mark in these two pericopes [about Herod in Mark 6:14-29 and about Pilate in Mark 15:1-15] is quite different. Power is represented as a network of relationships and expected behaviors in which a complex set of actors are engaged. . . . Reading both passages the message comes through that power is a web in which everybody is trapped, even those who supposedly rule.

Herod was a man conflicted. Similar entanglements will later prove to be Pilate's undoing as well (Mark 15:8-15). Both men will be caught up in corrupting webs of desire, social relations, power, and concern for their reputations.

So it turns out that Moreau was wrong. The apparition that most disturbs Herod is the social network that now entraps him into a bondage that is invisible to the eye, but fully public in its consequences. Now with the head of John before him, Herod must realize that it is that net — and his inability to do what is right despite the consequences — that have cost him his soul, the ghosts that haunt his waking psychological nightmare.

John, by contrast, was a man with a single message — the urgency of the Kingdom of God, and the unflinching demand that we live our lives in light of the claim that Kingdom makes upon us.

Herod wanted it all. He wanted the privileges that go with power. He wanted his brother's wife. He wanted his wife's daughter. He wanted to preserve his reputation with his friends. He wanted the final say in how he would be remembered. He wanted to be remembered as a man of his word. He wanted to have his cake and eat it, too. And it was his inability to disentangle himself from the tug of these conflicted desires that stopped his ears and made him unable to hear the Word of God.

The opposite of simplicity isn't extravagance. It's confusion. Herod might have learned something from Søren Kierkegaard: Purity of Heart is to will one thing.

In the end, his wants were dashed. If he is remembered at all, it is as the moral idiot who was bested by a dancing girl and a conniving wife — the murderer of a holy man.

There is a parabolic sense, then, in this story, and it is in keeping with the gospel story as a whole: it pits the powerless and weak against the powerful and arbitrary by reminding us that power itself — deployed for anything other than the Kingdom of God — can be a trap. It pits John's purity of heart against the entanglements and corruptions of Herod's conflicted heart that wants it all and is willing to sell his soul to get it. In telling the story this way, the gospels set forth an entirely different ethic for the management of power.

The following passage is from Mark 9:

> And they came to Capernaum; and when he was in the house he asked them, "What were you discussing on the way?" But they were silent; for on the way they had discussed with one another who was the greatest. And he sat down and called the twelve; and he said to them, "If anyone would be first, he must be last of all and servant of all."

This is from Chapter 10:

> And Jesus called them to him and said to them, "You know that those who are supposed to rule over the Gentiles lord it over them, and their great men exercise authority over them. But it shall not be so among you; but whoever would be great among you must be your servant, and whoever would be first among you must be slave of all. For the Son of man also came not to be served but to serve, and to give his life as a ransom for many."

If both John and Jesus are remembered as moral giants, it is precisely because of their singleness of purpose — their Purity of Heart. It is expressed for us as a fierce defiance of anything that would thwart the work of God in the world, and as an unwillingness to compromise their deepest identities as servants in the Kingdom of God, even when faced with the ultimate choice of life or death itself.

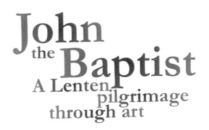

John
the Baptist
A Lenten
pilgrimage
through art

Behold
the Lamb of God
who takes away
the sin
of the world!

Behold
the Lamb of God
who takes away
the sin
of the world!

The Crucifixion of Jesus

Matthias Grünewald
The Crucifixion (panel from the Isenheim altarpiece)
1515 | oil on wood | 105 7/8 x 120 7/8 inches
Musee d'Unterlinden | Colmar

We close our pilgrimage by returning briefly to the major plot that gives the Baptist's story its meaning. We pick up the gospel at the scene of the crucifixion of Jesus. Historically, John has been dead now for perhaps three years, yet in the work of Matthias Grünewald (c.1475-1528, Germany), he joins us once again for this final reflection. On the left of the cross we find the traditional grouping of mourners — Mary Magdalene, identified by an ointment bottle, her own traditional emblem. Jesus' mother Mary, dressed in white, collapses into the arms of John the Beloved Disciple.

Jesus' body hangs upon the cross, distended and brutalized in death. Although his head hangs limp, his hands still claw heavenward. Even in death he reaches for his Father, as though the Father is here *in absentia*; it is the cry of dereliction enacted in fingertips. Placarded above his head are the letters I•N•R•I — Iesus Nazarenus Rex Iudaeorum — *Jesus of Nazareth, The King of the Jews*. Thus the Kingdom John proclaimed has finally come. The cross itself groans under the weight of the sins of the world.

What makes this image distinctive is that Grünewald has covered Jesus' body with ulcerated sores and boils. The scene was painted for the hospital of the Monastery of St Anthony, a center for the care of those sick with skin diseases.

Perhaps unwittingly, Grünewald has indicated two different dimensions of the crucifixion — Christ as the savior of our sins, but also Christ the healer of our infirmities. In the eastern theological tradition, these two dimensions are sometimes identified: in the end, sin itself is a sickness of the soul, in need not only of forgiveness but also of healing.

Behold
the Lamb of God
who takes away
the sin
of the world!

On the right, the Baptist continues his ministry, even now pointing toward the Christ whose path he had come to prepare. We see his emblems at his feet — the lamb and the reed cross. The lamb, wounded, bleeds into a golden chalice, an emblem for the Eucharist.

In his left hand John holds a book, no doubt the Holy Scriptures, while

with his right hand he indicates the Christ. Art critics often call attention to the disproportion in the figures, most especially the massive index finger of John's right hand; thus Grünewald has reverted to the Medieval practice of indicating relative social or theological significance in the proportions of his composition.

Above John's right hand, Grünewald has lettered the words that form the heart of this Lenten pilgrimage:

HE MUST INCREASE; I MUST DECREASE.

ABOUT THE AUTHOR

Jerry Camery-Hoggatt holds a PhD in Early Christian Origins from Boston University. He is the author of two books on the Gospel of Mark, two on interpretive method, and one on the role of narratives in the spiritual journey. His research involves the narrative paradigm as a mode of theological reflection. His published works also include an historical novel set in 13th Century Wales, two Christmas novellas, a collection of short stories, an illustrated children's book, and an historical novel set in 1st Century Rome.

BOOKS BY JERRY CAMERY-HOGGATT

Reading the Good Book Well: A Guide to Biblical Interpretation

From the cover:
Here is a single, accessible volume that explains the basic vocabulary and logic of biblical interpretation, shows how the various methodologies can be a seamless interpretive model for exegesis, and then reflects carefully on the implications of that method for reading, teaching, reflection, and preaching.

Through common and practical examples, Jerry Camery-Hoggatt teaches students a way of reading that replicates the activities the biblical authors expected their readers would perform. Using a model that is applicable across linguistic boundaries, genres, and cultural contexts, this volume introduces hermeneutics, translation theory, and textual and form criticism -- the tools students need to read and interpret the Bible.

Speaking of God: Reading and Preaching the Word of God

Camery-Hoggatt understands the complex interaction between readers and biblical texts, and he has accomplished an astounding feat for biblical preachers. He has taken apart the Swiss watch of biblical interpretation, showing all the gears, levers, and flywheels and patiently explaining how each one operates. Then, even more amazingly, he has put the whole thing back together again and made it work, producing fascinating examples of the text-to-sermon process.

> --Thomas G. Long | Francis Landey Patton Professor of Preaching and Worship, Princeton Theological Seminary

This is an important resource for those concerned with the negotiation of meaning in biblical texts in the service of the people of God.

--Joel B. Green | Associate Professor of Theology, Boston College

. . . this study demonstrates that a reader-response approach has significant implications for both exegesis and exposition. Indeed, it helps link these two moments in the pastor's overall homiletical endeavor . . .

--W. Randolph Tate | Associate Professor of Theology, Evangel College

. . . ought to be required reading in every seminary homiletics class. Every church board would be well served by seeing that their pastor has a copy . . .

--Charles Hedrick | Professor of Religious Studies and Distinguished Scholar, Southwest Missouri State University

Full Life Bible Commentary: Mark

Jerry Camery-Hoggatt wrote the commentary on Mark for this volume.

Numerous Bible commentaries have been written from a standard evangelical viewpoint. To date, however, no commentary exists that helps the reader examine the Bible from a Spirit-filled perspective. This New Testament commentary fills a long-standing need. In one exhaustive volume, the finest theologians and prominent authors from Pentecostal and moderate charismatic traditions unlock the Scriptures to present thoughtful insights into the entire New Testament, from Matthew through Revelation. Designed as a reader's companion, whether for serious Bible study or added enrichment to quiet times, the *Full Life Bible Commentary--New Testament* draws on the New International Version for its commentaries, but may be used with any favorite Bible translation. Filled with maps and charts, this volume presents a scholarly, accessible, and reasonable approach to the Bible that will yield rewards to Pentecostals, charismatics, and non-Pentecostals alike.

Good News in a Time of Trouble: A Readers' Commentary on the Gospel of Mark

An independently published version of the commentary on Mark from *Full Life Bible Commentary*. This commentary pays special attention to the processes involved in reading. It follows the interpretive method as set out in *Reading the Good Book Well* and *Speaking of God*.

Irony in Mark's Gospel: Text and Subtext

In recent years, an increasing number of interpreters have found dramatic and verbal ironies widely distributed in Mark's Gospel. This lucid study makes an important contribution to our understanding of Mark's irony and combines a literary-critical approach with insights gained from the sociology of knowledge. Professor Camery-Hoggatt argues that Mark's ironies are intentional, and that irony comprises an integral factor in Mark's overall strategy of composition: irony is a subtle means to achieve apologetic and paradigmatic ends.

Coffee Shop Spirituality: How What We Say to Each Other Over Coffee Can Deepen Or Damage Our Spiritual Lives

Gossip has always been an integral part of community, but in our Christian communities and homes, gossip becomes even more important. How can seemingly small disagreements end in a painful church split? Why does one sibling turn out to be the lost sheep and another the poster child? This book shows that more than any one factor, our gossip controls the spiritual climate of our churches, communities, and homes. *Coffee Shop Spirituality* exposes the destructive power of everyday, ordinary talk, but also shows the way to healing, uplifting, grace-full gossip.

Between the Monk and the Dragon: A Parable

A sixteen-year-old girl named Elspeth wakes one night to find a hatchling dragon in her father's bed. Elspeth's father, a hunter named John Fletcher, tells her she's had a bad dream, one she must not tell anyone about. Things deteriorate. The dragon reappears, each time growing in size and potency. As this happens, her father becomes increasingly angry, then violent. This is the story of their journey into family violence, and then out again. A monk at the local monastery, Constantine, a man who has had his own firsthand experience of violence, facilitates the outward journey. But within his care there lurks another danger: Constantine has a dragon of his own. It is a titanic struggle between forces both within and without. As she struggles with the other characters and with the dragon, Elspeth must learn the difficult lesson that forgiveness is the path to her own healing.

When Mother Was Eleven Foot-Four: A Christmas Memory

"This is the story of the Christmas of 1963, which is the Christmas that I learned what it means to be a giver of gifts."

In a beautifully written holiday memoir, the author tells the story of his mother, whose romantic nature and love for Christmas left a lifelong impression on her son. From her, he learns that sometimes you need to give what "your head tells you you can't afford, and your heart tells you you can't do without."

Mother has always celebrated Christmas with a flourish. So when she loses the Christmas spirit, her three young sons work hard to remind her what the season is about. The way her astounded reaction turned a corner for the family is something the author has never forgotten.

And neither will you. With vivid characters who are as timeless as the message, this delightful story will become a treasured part of your holiday traditions.

This story is also found in *Giver of Gifts*.

When Mother Was Eleven Foot-Four: A Christmas Memory (Illustrated Children's Version)

"When everything was ready, Pudge got to turn on the lights . . . and all at once, like magic . . . it was Christmas." Mother was only four-foot-eleven-inches tall on the outside, but when she was at her best she stood eleven-foot-four on the inside. And every Christmas she was at her best. Mother would carefully decorate a twelve-foot Christmas tree and load extravagant presents beneath its branches, and the magic of the holiday would begin. Then one year, everything changed. Mother cried on Christmas. As her sons tried to encourage her, they learned what it means to give good gifts--to be eleven-foot-four on the inside. *When Mother Was Eleven-Foot-Four* is beautifully illustrated and masterfully written for children ages four through eight and anyone young at heart. Your family will treasure it each year as a heart-warming story of hope and grace--a reminder that Christmas is a celebration of God's extravagant gift to us.

Jerry Camery-Hoggatt is Emeritus Professor of New Testament and Narrative Theology at Vanguard University in Costa Mesa, California. He loves writing and preaching, but more than anything he loves telling stories. He takes special joy in discovering the ways God complicates our plots in an artful play to turn us into more interesting and Christlike characters.

Mark Elliott illustrated the children's picture book classic *Candle in the Window* and numerous young adult book covers, including the Newbery-Award-winning series *The Princess Tales*. He lives on a working sheep farm in the lower Hudson Valley along with two donkeys and two crazy long-haired cats.

Giver of Gifts: Three Stories of Christmas Grace

The magic of the season wrapped in three timeless tales. Beautifully written and unique, these memorable stories celebrate Christmas in three very different ways. Each well-crafted tale by this masterful storyteller illuminates the heart of generosity, the beauty of grace, and the wonder of hope. Travel back to Jesus's birth and discover the tender blessings of his earthly father. Witness the transformation of a young girl as she begins to see others in a gentler light. And learn to be an extravagant giver of gifts from a mother who's tiny in stature but big in Christmas spirit. *Giver of Gifts* offers stories you will want to read again year after year. Using the power of story, it serves as a reminder of what it means to give--and live--with a generous and gracious heart.

My Mother's Wish: An American Christmas Carol

"An enchanted, stirring tale about the greatest and most surprising gifts, acceptance and love."

–Elizabeth Dewberry │ Author of *His Lovely Wife, Sacrament of Lies*, and *Break the Heart of Me*

"Over the years I've read about every conceivable kind of Christmas story that existed. Then came this one: truly a wondrous one-of-a-kind tale bringing laughter and tears. If it were possible to fuse the writing styles and messages of Garrison Keillor, C. S. Lewis, Dave Barry, and Catherine Marshall, the result might very well bear the title *My Mother's Wish*."

–Joe L. Wheeler, PhD │ Editor of the *Christmas In My Heart®* story anthology series

"Jerry Camery-Hoggatt explores the mystical relationship that binds mothers and children together and gives all of us an opportunity to revisit that magical time as our own mothers dragged us, kicking and screaming at times, through childhood. This is a book that makes you think—and remember. You will want to call and thank your own mother and tell her you love her."

> —Ed Butchart | Professional and official Santa, Stone Mountain, Georgia, and author of *Red Suit Diaries* and *More Red Suit Diaries*

"Eleanor Crumb McKutcheon—call her Ellee, please—is a precocious little tweener blessed with a ratty wryness that puts her at odds with her purposeful mother, whose heavenly vision of what her daughter should be bears no resemblance whatever to what Ellie sees for herself. When hostilities reach epic proportions, Ellie packs up and leaves, an act of rebellion and defiance that brings her, kicking and screaming, into the neighborhood of grace. Jerry Camery-Hoggatt's charming Christmas fable is proof that a less-than-accommodating Bethlehem stable still has room for every last one of us."

> —Dr. James Calvin Schaap | Department of English, Dordt College, author of *Startling Joy* and *Romey's Place*

Made in United States
Orlando, FL
20 March 2022

15963289R00100